To My Countrywomen

The Life of Sarah Josepha Hale

by
Muriel L. Dubois

Apprentice Shop Books, LLC
Bedford, New Hampshire
© 2006

Apprentice Shop Books, LLC
Bedford, New Hampshire

Text copyright ©2006

All illustrations from the author's private collection.

For information regarding permissions contact:
Apprentice Shop Books, LLC
7 Colby Court, Box 156
Bedford, NH 03110

LIBRARY OF CONGRESS CATALOGING-IN PUBLICATION DATA

Dubois, Muriel L.
    To My Countrywomen: The Life of Sarah Josepha Hale/
    by Muriel L. Dubois;
Summary: A biography of Sarah Josepha Buell Hale, the first woman editor in the United States, writer, and activist for women's education. Includes bibliography.

ISBN 0-9723410-1-3

1. Hale, Sarah Josepha 1788 – 1879—Juvenile literature. 2. Women editors—United States—biography—Juvenile literature. 3. Women writers—19th century—United States—Juvenile literature. 4. Women activists—19th century—United States—Juvenile literature

Oceanic Graphic Printing, Inc.
105 Main Street, Hackensack, NJ 07601

Printed in China

On the cover: Portrait of Sarah Hale from *Women's Record or; Sketches of Distinguished Women*, 1873.

Cover design and book design by Lisa Greenleaf
www.greenleafdesignstudio.com

Contents

Dedication

To my parents, Roger and Laurette Major,
who always encouraged me to read and learn
as much as I could; and to their mothers,
Delia Major and Josephine Bourque
and all the strong women in our
family who came before them.

To My Countrywomen

The Life of Sarah Josepha Hale

"Mary had a little lamb,
Its fleece was white as snow.
And everywhere that Mary went,
The lamb was sure to go..."

Almost everyone knows that rhyme. Almost no one knows who wrote it. Even fewer people know that the author was a woman who lived during the 1800s. Her legacy is much more than a few lines of a children's rhyme. She championed causes that changed laws and attitudes affecting men, women, and children. Her extensive writings altered American lives.

Newport, New Hampshire was a small farming community.
The Sugar River crossed the town and connected
to nearby Lake Sunapee.

Chapter One
Newport, New Hampshire
1805 – 1813

Sarah Josepha was born on October 24, 1788 to Martha and Gordon Buell. She was the third child and eldest daughter of the farmer and his wife. Five years later, Sarah's only sister, Martha, was born.

Sarah grew into a beautiful young woman. She had dark brown hair and soft, hazel eyes.

The day that set the tone for Sarah Buell's life work occurred when she was just seventeen. In late summer, 1805, she watched her brother Horatio leave their home in Newport, New Hampshire. Horatio, just a year older than Sarah, was on his way to Dartmouth College to study law.

Sarah wished she could follow her brother. They had always studied together and challenged each other. But now Sarah was left behind. It did not matter that she loved learning and studying as much as Horatio did.

Dartmouth College did not accept women students. Sarah did not know any college that did. Too many people still believed that women's brains were smaller than men's brains and not meant for "intellectual learning." Sarah was grateful that her mother, Martha, had never gone along with that silly, old-fashioned idea. Mrs. Buell had always encouraged both of her daughters as well as her two sons to learn as much as they could.

Mrs. Buell had taken on most of the responsibility for the education of her four children. Charles, Horatio, Sarah, and young Martha read from the Bible, and John Bunyan's *The Pilgrim's Progress*. She encouraged her children to write essays and read everything they could.

Sarah was especially fond of a book called *History of the American Revolution*. Her father, then Captain Gordon Buell, had been wounded in America's War for Independence. He'd fought under the great General George Washington himself. Sarah understood the sacrifices these men had made for freedom. She loved to read stories about America's heroes.

Sarah remembered how amazed she had been when her mother lent her a novel that was popular in Europe. It was not just the plot of *The Mysteries of Udolpho* that had impressed Sarah. She was much more taken with the book's author. Later, Sarah would comment on her childhood impressions:

> ...of all the books I saw, few were written by Americans, and none by women. Here was a work, the most fascinating I had ever read excepting 'The Pilgrims' Progress," written by a woman! How happy it made me!

The author was not only a woman, but also a *married* woman. There was her name, right on the leaf: Mrs. Ann Ward Radcliffe. *Mrs.* Radcliffe. The implication was that even her husband approved of her work. The idea was incredible, shocking! But it also gave Sarah courage. She continued to write stories, essays, and poems. If someone like Mrs. Radcliffe could write a novel, perhaps Sarah could be a writer, too.

Charles, Sarah's oldest brother, was away at sea when Horatio left for Dartmouth. Now, with both Buell boys gone, the remaining family members would have to make adjustments.

Sarah planned changes for her own life. She spread the word among her neighbors. She would open a "dame school." Dame schools prepared young children to attend the regular town school. Four and five-year-old children learned their letters and numbers. They learned to read a little. Girls practiced sewing. Boys studied some math.

Boys attended a dame school until they were old enough to sit still for the schoolmaster. Girls could stay longer or attend the town school. Sarah's plan was to teach traditional lessons with some new ideas of her own. She intended to teach her young neighbors just as her own mother had taught her and her siblings.

Like her mother, Sarah believed little children loved to learn and teachers should take advantage of this natural love of learning. The young ones that gathered with Sarah were barely more than toddlers. They practiced their alphabet. Sarah taught them to recognize numbers and count. She helped the students learn to read and write, and she insisted that the girls study as much math as the boys. She even introduced her young students to the study of Latin! Working with the children helped Sarah put aside her own frustrations about not being allowed to attend college.

Historians believe Sarah ran her little school for about four years. There is no record of exactly where Sarah held her school. Some scholars believe the school existed in a part of Newport called "the Guild." That would mean Sarah's school was not located in the family's farmhouse.

Meanwhile, Horatio did not forget his younger sister's disappointment. Whenever he came home from college, he brought along his textbooks. He and Sarah sat together as they had when they were children. Horatio reviewed everything he had learned during the semester. Sarah pored over the texts, asking questions and arguing ideas with her brother. Later in her life, Sarah loved to tell people that thanks to Horatio, she had managed to receive a thorough college education. She just did not have the diploma to prove it.

In 1810, the Buell family sold their farm. They moved to the village center. Mr. Buell had been farming in Newport for nearly twenty years. But he was in poor health and, without his boys' help, farm work became too much. The captain had suffered war wounds during his time as a soldier. He never completely recovered from them. It was time to try work that would be less physically demanding. Sarah's father decided to open a tavern.

A 19th century tavern was a combination restaurant, hotel, and post office. People gathered there to get the town news. Newcomers rented rooms until they could settle into their own homes. Mail coaches dropped and collected letters and packages. Sarah, then twenty-two, and her seventeen-year-old sister helped their parents run the Rising Sun Tavern.

A year after Gordon Buell opened the tavern, a young lawyer came to Newport. His name was David Hale. He planned to practice law in the growing town. Like many other newcomers, David rented a room at the Rising Sun while he set up his office and looked for permanent lodging.

David and Sarah became good friends. They had much in common. They both loved to read and study. Best of all, David believed, as Sarah's family did, that women as well as men should learn as much as they could.

David's friendship was important to Sarah in 1811. She needed his strength and support. That year was very tragic for the Buell family. First, they learned that Charles had been lost at sea. In the fall, young Martha developed tuberculosis and died. Just a few months later, on Christmas Day, Sarah's mother also died.

Captain Buell was heartsick from the loss of his wife and children. The sadness he experienced made his health worse. Only Sarah was left to help her father run the Rising Sun. The next year, Captain Buell sold the tavern, but he and Sarah continued to rent rooms there.

Sarah and David fell in love but they did not marry for two more years. Sarah wrote little about this period in her life. It was customary for a family to be in mourning for at least a year following a family member's death. During that time, a young woman like Sarah might wear dark clothing. She would not attend social functions and would remain at home for much of the time. Sarah, as the hostess of the Rising Sun until its sale, would not have had the luxury of closing herself off from the public during this difficult time. She and her father would have continued caring for their guests and earning their livelihood.

Perhaps Sarah felt a great responsibility to stay by her father's side until he became stronger. Perhaps David Hale, still a fairly new business owner, was not ready to support a family. For whatever reason, David and Sarah delayed their wedding date.

Chapter Two

Family Life
1813 – 1822

On Saturday October 23, 1813, the day before her twenty-fifth birthday, Sarah Buell married David Hale. The ceremony was held at the Rising Sun Tavern, Sarah's home for three years and the place where she met David, the love of her life.

While we do not know exactly what that day was like, we can make some guesses. Sarah often wrote about weddings and romance. She may have described a ceremony very similar to her own. Nineteenth century marriage ceremonies were held at home or in a church. Families might gather for a private meal in someone's home or merely serve tea and cake. Sarah was a small town farm girl. Her later writings show her to be a practical person who did not believe in wasting money on frills. Sarah did not have a mother or sister to help her plan the day. Sarah's father was not well and the Buells still mourned those who had died. It was likely that the Hales' wedding was a very simple affair.

Sarah might have followed the tradition of wearing a new dress that would become her "best" dress. After the wedding, Sarah would wear the dress for church services or special occasions. Sarah and David's celebration was probably small and quiet. Captain

Buell, a few close friends, and some of David's family members may have witnessed the brief ceremony.

We do not know if Horatio Buell attended his sister's wedding. After college, Horatio moved to New York State to practice law. He later became a judge in Glens Falls.

Sarah and David's wedding day marked the beginning of an especially happy period. The Hales bought a home in Newport and David continued to practice law. A young woman in Sarah's position was expected to care for her home and husband, and to do good works for people who were less fortunate. Married women did not have careers. But Sarah's life with David was bit unusual.

Sarah later described this period in her life. Each evening the young husband and wife devoted two hours to reading and writing. Sarah cherished that special time of day. "Two hours out of twenty-four. How I enjoyed those hours!" she wrote.

David recommended books for them to read and discuss. He encouraged Sarah to write poems and stories. David was proud of Sarah's writing talent. He sent some of her poems to local newspapers for publication. Later, Sarah and some friends began a writers' group, the Newport Coterie. The women submitted their work for publication, but did not use their real names if their pieces were printed. Many women of the period did not want to appear too proud by publicizing their names. Sarah often used the pen name "Cornelia" in her published work.

In 1815, two years after their marriage, Sarah gave birth to the Hales' first son. They named him David, after his father. Their second son was born in 1817. Horatio was named for his uncle. Even as their young family grew, David and Sarah continued their ritual of reading, writing, and discussion.

In the fall of 1818, when Sarah was expecting her third child, she became gravely ill. Doctors believed that Sarah had contracted tuberculosis. Like her younger sister, Martha, she was expected to die. At that time, doctors believed that tuberculosis, or consumption as they called it, was a result of poisons in the body.

The only way to cure it, they thought, was to rid the body of the poisons. They did this by blood-letting (cutting the patient to force her to bleed) or by giving the patient drugs that would cause vomiting. They kept patients indoors, afraid that the outside air would further weaken them. Doctors in the early 1800s did not realize that these techniques might actually make

the patient's health worse.

David Hale did not accept the doctors' opinions. Perhaps he remembered how little these treatments did for Sarah's sister. Perhaps he felt he had nothing to lose by taking matters into his own hands. He decided he must try to save the life of his young wife. He left the boys in the care of family members and took Sarah to the mountains.

The New Hampshire mountain air is cool, clear, and crisp in the fall. Many well-to-do people rode north to escape the heat of the towns, to relax, or hike. Horse-drawn coaches carried travelers to mountain inns and grand hotels. The northern forests were thick with dark green shade and wildflowers. Purple grapes were ripe and ready to be picked. David insisted that Sarah rest and eat the fruit. On clear, sunny days Sarah relaxed in the sunshine. Every day she and David took coach rides along the mountain roads.

Tuberculosis is a serious lung disease. Patients who survived took many months to heal from it. It is possible that Sarah did not have this illness but some other lung infection. Doctors of the period might have called many similar lung diseases, such as bronchitis, "consumption." For whatever reason, David's ideas succeeded. Slowly, Sarah began to regain her strength. All her life Sarah believed this "grape cure" had saved her. Later, she insisted on having grapes available whenever they could be purchased.

After six weeks, Sarah returned home feeling much stronger and healthier. She gave birth to her first daughter, Frances Ann, the following spring. Sadly, Sarah's father, Captain Buell, died just weeks later. Now only she and her brother, Horatio, remained of the original Buell family. Because Horatio lived in New York, visits between the siblings were rare.

During the next three years, the Hales became more established in their community. David Hale's law practice grew. He became a respected member of the local Masonic Lodge. Sometimes called the Freemasons, this organization of Christian men performed charitable works for those in need. Their good deeds especially were aimed at the elderly, widows, and orphans.

In 1820, Sarah and David welcomed a second daughter, Sarah Josepha. The family called her Josepha. If Sarah's life had continued in this manner, she would have simply been one of many anonymous 19th century wives and mothers. Her name, or the

name "Cornelia," might have appeared occasionally under the title of a poem or story submitted to a local newspaper. Few people would have known her or known about her views. Instead, Sarah's life changed dramatically.

Sarah was expecting her fifth child in September of 1822 when David Hale was called out of town on business. There was nothing unusual about the trip as David often traveled for trials. But on his way home, David was caught in a snowstorm—uncommon for September in New Hampshire. Even in the northeast, warm, gentle weather often lingers through the fall. Morning frosts do not appear until the harvests of October and November. David, therefore, had not expected the cold and snow and was not dressed for it.

He drove his carriage on, struggling through the wet, freezing weather. A New Englander would know the folly of stopping where there was no shelter. While the trip might take longer, it was best to keep moving. When David Hale finally reached Newport, he was nearly frozen. He became seriously ill from the exposure he suffered. He died of pneumonia on September 25, 1822.

The Hales had been married for only nine years. Sarah became a widow at thirty-four years of age. She had four children to care for and a fifth child soon to be born. Although David had been a successful lawyer, he had not been in business long enough to put away much in savings. There would be no more income from David's law practice. It was now up to Sarah to see that her young family survived.

Chapter Three
Sarah Carries On
1823 – 1827

Sarah was left alone to raise five children. The oldest was only seven years old. Two were still toddlers. A new baby was expected within weeks. And soon there would be no money left.

Sarah sorted through her few possible options. American society placed many restrictions on her ability to earn a living. She thought about her life experiences. She had been an innkeeper, a teacher, and a farm girl. The Rising Sun was sold. Sarah could not go back to teaching since only men or unmarried women were allowed to be teachers. Even if the school district made an exception in Sarah's case, the amount paid to women teachers was less than the amount paid to the schoolmasters. It would not be enough to care for Sarah's family. Farming was not a reasonable choice for a woman alone with five young children.

Baby William arrived just weeks after his father's death. Friends and neighbors did not forget the Hales.

David Hale, along with other members of the Freemasons, had once done charitable work. Now David's family was in need. Members of his Masonic Lodge helped to set Sarah up in business. She and her sister-in-law, Hannah Hale, opened a millinery shop in

Newport. The Hale ladies sold hats and other women's clothing. The solution was a good one. Since Sarah had helped her father run the Rising Sun Tavern, she was an experienced businesswoman. She knew how to deal with the public. And, with her sister-in-law's help, Sarah could still care for her new baby while she worked at the store.

But Sarah did not like being a shopkeeper. At night, when the shop was closed and her children were asleep, Sarah kept up the custom she had shared with David. She devoted two hours each evening to reading and writing. Writing gave Sarah an outlet for her grief. She wrote dozens of poems and began to work on a novel. Through her poetry Sarah described her fears, expressed her gratitude, and wept for the child who never knew his father:

> Oh! Cease that plaint, my babe, no father's ear
> Is open to thy wail, thy mother's tear,
> Her helpless tears may bathe thy cheek, but she,
> As sorrow's heir can only welcome thee…

The poems could have been kept as a personal collection. Perhaps Sarah would have shown them only to close friends and family members. But, once again,

the men of David's Masonic lodge came to Sarah's aid.

The members knew about Sarah's writing abilities. With their financial help, she published a collection of her work called *The Genius of Oblivion and Other Original Poems.* In keeping with the tradition of those times, Sarah's name did not appear as author. Women writers were still very much a minority. Sarah may have felt it was too boastful for a lady, particularly a widow, to bring attention to herself in that way. Perhaps she feared the book would fail. For whatever reason, the author simply was listed as "A Lady from New Hampshire."

The Genius of Oblivion contained narrative poems and other, more personal poems addressed to family and friends. Sarah did not forget David's lodge members and all their help. The first poem in the book, "Dedication," expressed Sarah's gratitude to her sponsors:

"...My Friends, my Patrons, bless with life and love,
With hope below, and happiness above...
...your patronage shall be my boast—
You kindly gave it when 'twas needed most."

The little books sold very well. Sarah was encouraged. She began to think that she might even be able to earn her living as a writer. She continued to submit stories and poems to various periodicals. Eventually, enough newspapers and magazines bought Sarah's work so she could leave the millinery store in Hannah's hands.

Even as Sarah wrote short pieces for newspapers, magazines, and poetry collections, she kept working on a novel: *Northwood, or, Life North and South*. The book was very unusual for that time. More than twenty years had passed since Sarah had read Mrs. Radcliffe's *The Mysteries of Udolpho*, yet little had changed for women writers. Few American women had published novels. In addition, the United States was experiencing a period of great disagreement.

Many states in the South depended on slave labor to work their large farms. Many people in the northern states wanted slavery to end. *Northwood* was one of the first novels to include the institution of slavery in its plot. Sarah's book told, in great detail, about life in the northern and southern parts of the United States.

Sarah had grown up hearing about the sacrifices men like her father had made to free and unite the original thirteen colonies. She had an unwavering love for the young republic. But she could see that as the United

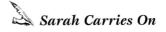

NORTHWOOD;

OR,

LIFE NORTH AND SOUTH:

SHOWING THE

TRUE CHARACTER OF BOTH.

BY

MRS. SARAH JOSEPHA HALE.

Illustrated

" HE WHO LOVES NOT HIS COUNTRY CAN LOVE NOTHING."

———————

NEW YORK:
H. LONG & BROTHER,
48 ANN-STREET.

Sarah Hale's first novel, Northwood, *compared life in the North and South after the American Revolution.*

States expanded, differences between the North and South also grew.

The North was becoming a center for manufacturing. Factories and mills built along the rivers of such towns as Pawtucket, Rhode Island and Manchester, New Hampshire produced miles of cotton and wool cloth each day. People left their farms to work in the factory towns. Millwork gave them a chance to earn regular pay.

The South, with its warmer weather and longer growing season, continued to be a center for farming. Its vast plantations needed hundreds of workers. Slavery was a cheap way to get these workers.

Slavery had existed in the northern states, too. But the North had little financial reason to keep up the practice. Most northern states began outlawing slavery after the Revolutionary War.

An anti-slavery movement called abolitionism was becoming stronger—particularly in the North. In the meantime, an inventor named Eli Whitney produced a machine that made slavery even more profitable in the South. Whitney's cotton gin quickly cleaned sticks, seeds, and dirt from harvested cotton bolls. Farmers sold more cotton, but also needed more slaves to plant

and harvest the crops.

The North and South had once been united in their desire to be free of England's control. Now they disagreed more and more with each other. Sarah, like many other Americans, feared these arguments would one day lead to war.

Northwood addressed these issues. In the novel, Sarah reminded her fellow citizens of their common roots. She tried to inspire feelings of unity and patriotism that might help overcome the growing differences between the states. Sarah tried to present a balanced view of citizens in both the north and the south. The novel was published in Boston in 1827, and it became an immediate best seller. It was even reprinted in Great Britain as, *A New England Tale.*

While it was a financial success, *Northwood* did not fulfill one of Sarah's hopes. It did not bring about unified feeling between the states. The national disagreements continued.

But the book's success led to one important, if more personal, result: *Northwood* opened the door to Sarah's future. A gentleman named Reverend John L. Blake was especially impressed with Sarah's work. Reverend Blake planned to publish a woman's magazine. The idea of a magazine written specifically for women was a new one in the United States. A few English publishers had produced women's magazines but American magazines were written primarily for men. They sometimes included one or two articles directed at women. Blake intended his magazine to be devoted entirely to women's interests.

Reverend Blake wanted an educated woman to be the editor of his new *Ladies Magazine.* He lived in Boston but had once belonged to a Masonic Lodge in Concord, New Hampshire and had heard of Sarah Hale. Now, with the success of *Northwood,* John Blake felt he had found just the editor he needed.

He wrote to Sarah and asked her to consider taking the position. As part of the deal, Reverend Blake wanted Sarah to move to Boston where he intended to publish *Ladies Magazine.* The job seemed like a great opportunity, but Sarah did not accept immediately. She first thought about its impact on her children. She wondered if it would be in her children's best interests to uproot them and rearrange their lives.

The regular pay she would receive as an editor would certainly help her family—but only if the magazine succeeded. Many people still believed that

women did not need to be educated. Also, most state laws said that all of a woman's money belonged to her husband or guardian. The success of *Ladies Magazine* depended on men allowing their wives, daughters, or sisters to buy it.

Sarah considered all of these points as she decided what answer she would give John Blake.

Chapter Four

New Challenges
1827 – 1828

Sarah had been offered the job of a lifetime. She had the opportunity to support her children doing the thing she loved most to do—write. She was excited about the idea of a magazine devoted entirely to women. Ideas for stories and articles filled her mind. *Ladies Magazine* could champion education for women. Sarah could review new books and showcase short stores and poems written by women. The magazine could include homemaking hints and opinions about raising children.

But Sarah separated ambition from dreams. She knew that she had to consider the practical side of Reverend Blake's offer. The magazine was a financial risk. John Blake would be trying to sell subscriptions to a group that, for the most part, did not control its own money.

More than the concern over the success or failure of *Ladies Magazine,* Sarah worried about her children. They had always lived in Newport. Their lives already had been transformed by their father's sudden death. Moving to Boston would mean leaving their home, their friends, and familiar surroundings. Sarah wondered if she could risk disrupting their lives so much. What

if the magazine failed? Would she be able to return to Newport? Or would she and her children be left alone and without support in Boston?

After much thought and discussion, Sarah decided she could not uproot her children when so many factors were unknown. The job would help her support her family, but who would care for the children while she worked? She accepted Reverend Blake's offer—with one condition. She asked to delay the move to Boston for several months.

Within a year, Sarah's oldest son, fourteen-year-old David, would enter West Point Military Academy. He would board at the school and could come to Boston between terms. Five-year-old William could live in Boston with his mother. The middle children were Sarah's greatest concern. Sarah's second son, Horatio, her brother's namesake, was only eleven. Frances and Josepha attended Miss Fiske's Young Ladies Seminary in nearby Keene.

Family members offered their help. Once Sarah was ready to go to Boston, the middle children would live with uncles and aunts. Sarah's brother, Horatio, and his wife, Elizabeth, offered to care for their nephew. The girls would live with her husband's brother, Salma, and wife, during the school term.

John Blake agreed to allow Sarah to edit the first few issues of the magazine from Newport. During that time, he and Sarah could see whether the magazine would succeed. Sarah was ready to work.

Sarah wanted *Ladies Magazine* to teach women all sorts of new and useful things. She implemented her ideas immediately. Along with household hints, stories and poems, Sarah added pieces about America's history.

But Sarah also understood she had a huge hurdle to overcome. She must appeal to the men who controlled each family's money. This would be a challenge. A year's subscription for *Ladies Magazine* was set at $3.00—a considerable sum for the average household to spend on an unnecessary item. Sarah knew it wouldn't do any good to belittle men or their role as head of the house. That method would only turn away potential sales. Instead, she had to show men that *Ladies Magazine* would help their families.

Editors usually write a short piece, called an editorial, at the beginning of a magazine. The editorial is meant to interest the reader in the magazine's contents. It often highlights some of the articles that appear in that issue. Sarah began the first issue of

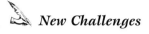

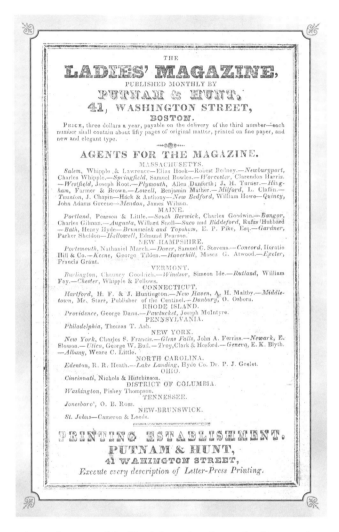

An early copy of Ladies Magazine shows the $3.00 price and indicates that the magazine was sold throughout New England, the South, and parts of Canada.

Ladies Magazine with an editorial. But she did not merely introduce the new publication. Sarah addressed her first editorial to the men.

She pointed out than an educated woman was a much more interesting woman. Mothers, Sarah pointed out, were their children's first teachers. The new magazine would help "...mothers be competent to the task of instructing their children..." She suggested that educated children brought glory to their country, so buying *Ladies Magazine* would be an act of patriotism. These were modern, risky ideas, but they worked! The magazine became an immediate success.

Now Sarah could begin to dream as well as plan. If the magazine continued to be successful, Sarah thought, she would have a dependable way to support herself and the children. She daydreamed of remaining an editor for ten years. By the end of that time, most of her children's schooling would be complete. Then she would have only herself to care for.

For the most part, women readers loved the new magazine. But they hoped to find one more thing in the pages of *Ladies Magazine:* fashion plates. These sketches showed three or four of the latest dress designs from Europe. Women readers wrote to the "lady editor"

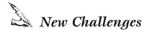

Boston City Hall in the early 1800s. Moving to a major city like Boston was a dramatic change for Sarah Hale.

and her publisher requesting the addition of the plates. American women wanted to be stylish.

Sarah had definite opinions about clothing and beauty. She often wrote about these topics in her articles and editorials. She believed a woman should dress comfortably in clothing that suited her. Women would be more beautiful if they ate healthy foods and exercised instead of merely trying to look fashionable.

For these reasons, Sarah did not feel the need to include fashion plates in *Ladies Magazine*. But Sarah would learn that her readers were just as stubborn as she was.

For several months, Sarah continued to edit the magazine from her home in New Hampshire. She felt relief and gratitude for the turn her life had taken. So many horrible things could have happened after David's death. In the early 1800s, widowed mothers did not have the government and social help that people have today. Women who could not support their children often had to give the younger ones up. Sometimes, wealthy people were willing to adopt the babies. Older children were sent out to work or to orphanages. Sarah understood how lucky she and her children were. All of the Hale children would continue their schooling.

Once it appeared that the magazine was going to succeed, Sarah kept her promise to John Blake. She prepared to leave Newport for Boston.

Chapter Five

Mrs. Hale, Editress
1829 – 1830

Twenty-four years after watching her brother, Horatio, leave for college, it was Sarah's turn to say goodbye to Newport. The trip to Boston was long and tiring. Few roads were paved and coaches often needed repair during such trips. Sarah's coach traveled over rutted dirt roads as it headed south to the seacoast.

Nineteenth century Boston was one of the most important seaports in the world. How different the hustle and bustle must have seemed to Sarah after all her years in quiet Newport!

Sarah and William moved into a boarding house on Central Court. One of Sarah's first projects was to hire a teacher for William. She asked the teacher to find several other students who could be taught along with William. The little boy was not used to being without his brothers and sisters. William's classmates would become his new playmates, too.

Sarah had not lived in Boston for long before she observed major differences in the lives of Boston's citizens. While some people lived in extreme wealth, others—like the families of the sailors who helped make Boston a great seaport—lived in terrible poverty. Many sailors' wives were left alone for months or years at a time as their husbands traveled around the world.

These women struggled to care for their homes and children. The wives often were left with little money for clothing or food. They took terrible jobs that paid little. Sarah learned that many of them worked in "slop shops" making sailor's clothing. Slop shops were hot, dusty rooms where dozens of women crowded together to work. The women earned pennies for each article of clothing they sewed, but the items were then sold to sailors at a high price. Some sailors had to ask for their pay in advance so that they could buy the clothes they needed to work at sea. Their families were left in poverty while the men paid back the money they had borrowed. Many of these sailors' families lived in cramped, run-down homes but could afford nothing better. They were caught in a trap of poverty and disease.

Sarah remembered how much her family had missed her brother, Charles, when he left home. She recalled their horror when they learned that he had been lost at sea. Sarah, who had been left so suddenly with the care of her own five children, understood the needs of the sailors' wives. She wished to help these families and others just as she had been helped since David's death.

One of the first columns she wrote urged readers to support Boston's "Fatherless and Widows Society." She called widows and orphans "...the most forlorn and destitute of any class of people in the world..." The column was just the beginning. Sarah would continue to use *Ladies Magazine* as an instrument of charity. And she resolved to find ways to help the wives and children of working sailors.

Sarah saw, in *Ladies Magazine,* infinite possibilities for raising the status of women. But she knew women could not improve their lives without education. She began a regular series on schools for girls called "Female Seminaries." Sarah did not want her daughters or other young women to experience the disappointment and hurt she had faced the day Horatio left for Dartmouth. Attitudes about women's education were changing. More people seemed to believe that women should be allowed to attend college. More schools for young ladies—like the one her daughters attended in Keene— were opening up. Sarah wanted to make all women aware of the possibilities they and their daughters had to become better educated. One of the schools that Sarah wrote about was Emma Willard's Troy Female Seminary in New York. Sarah was impressed with the school's program and teachers. She wrote:

> "…Mrs. Willard shows her good sense; and
> the worth of those who manage the
> various departments of the school will…
> be… appreciated by all sensible people."

Mrs. Emma Willard

Sarah and Emma Willard, united in their belief in the education of women, became good friends. The women had much in common. They were only a year apart in age. Both had been encouraged by their families to read and learn as much as they could. Both had married men who had encouraged them to challenge their minds. Over the years, they often would work together for the cause of women's education. Later, both of Sarah's daughters would attend Mrs. Willard's school. Her younger daughter, Josepha, would receive her teaching certificate.

Another topic that Sarah included in the pages of *Ladies Magazine* had to do with women who worked outside the home. City women worked as servants, cooks, seamstresses, or labored in factories. Some women were forced to bring their children to the mills while they worked long hours. No laws protected the children from playing near the loud, dangerous factory machinery. No laws forced parents to find babysitters or send the children to school. The children of these women, Sarah wrote, needed proper care and teaching during the day. Many women in this situation had been raised in poverty and did not have the "...time and rarely the ability," Sarah said, to prepare their children for school. Sarah wrote essays urging that public infant schools (like today's day care centers and pre-schools) be developed and opened to any child. Such schools would give every child the opportunity to learn.

Sarah did not just suggest that mothers teach their children. She also offered ideas for books and lessons. By the second year of *Ladies Magazine's* publication, Sarah was already devoting pages of her "Literary Notices"—or book reviews—to critiques of new or important children's books.

Sarah used the magazine to encourage patriotism. Many of the stories and poems she chose or wrote for *Ladies Magazine* showed her love for the United States. Even as an adult, Sarah continued to revere the men, like her father, who had fought in the American Revolution. She was disappointed, therefore, to learn that the city of Boston failed to complete a project to honor the veterans of the first battle of the Revolutionary War: the Battle of Bunker Hill.

Major General Henry Dearborn had served as captain during the battle. His son, also named Henry, had proposed the idea for a monument in 1822. The stone memorial, shaped like an Egyptian obelisk, would be built near the site of the battle. No monument to the American Revolution existed in any other town or state. Many important men, including Congressman Daniel Webster and Harvard Professor Edward Everett became sponsors of the project. The organizers laid the monument's cornerstone on June 17, 1825 during a 50th anniversary celebration honoring the veterans of The War for Independence.

Five years later, construction stopped. No more money could be raised to complete the obelisk. Huge blocks of granite, surrounded by weeds, lay near the partly finished project. Sarah urged her readers to help:

> "…we would suggest that an attempt be
> made by the women of Massachusetts
> (or all of New England, if that be
> thought best) to raise…the sum of fifty
> thousand dollars…"

Many people laughed at the idea. If men—who controlled the finances—couldn't complete the project, what could women expect to do?

Sarah did not let this attitude stop her. She knew that 900,000 women lived in New England alone. If only one fourth of the ladies each gave twenty-five cents, more than fifty thousand dollars would be raised. Sarah did not only mention the plan in *Ladies Magazine*. She joined a Committee of Correspondence.

The members wrote personal letters to everyone they knew and asked for their help. Slowly the money began to trickle in. Sarah saw, firsthand, how influential *Ladies Magazine* could be. But while Sarah seemed to be helping to win this battle, she was losing another.

Women were still writing to the publisher and asking that the magazine include fashion plates. Sarah tried to point out in her editorials that even the women of Paris—where the plates came from—didn't wear the impossible styles. Emma Willard sided with Sarah. Mrs. Willard had recently returned from Europe. She had seen, first hand, the kind of clothing worn by the women of France. Sarah quoted Emma Willard in *Ladies Magazine:* "The French Ladies," Mrs. Willard wrote, "are not in dress what they are supposed in our country to be… their taste is chaste and correct."

But even someone as well-known and influential as Mrs. Willard could not change the public's attitude.

John Blake listened to his readers. He insisted that fashion plates become part of the magazine. Over Sarah's objections, the first plates were included in the November 1830 issue.

The first fashion plate published in Ladies Magazine
*featured the latest European dress designs
and some very unusual hair styles.*

Sarah's editorial for that month let her readers know just what she thought. She told her readers that women who followed styles, instead of dressing to suit their own bodies, were foolish. What's more, they dishonored the United States! Instead of buying from American seamstresses, Sarah wrote, we "…pay extravagant prices to the foreign milliner, merely because she made bonnets for a duchess…" But readers wouldn't give up the plates. Even in 1830 people were interested in what the rich and famous wore!

That fall Sarah learned that the her Bunker Hill Monument project had only raised three thousand dollars. That was not nearly enough to finish the obelisk. The committee voted to invest the money until a way could be found to raise more. Sarah was disheartened but not discouraged. Surely a group of intelligent, hard-working women could find a way to make the plan succeed.

In the meantime, there were other issues that needed to be brought before the public. *Ladies Magazine* was just the place to start.

Chapter Six

Busy Sarah
1831 – 1834

Some wealthy, influential people lived in Boston. Long-established families traced their roots to Boston's founders. Harvard College, across the Charles River, was one of America's most revered centers of learning. The young men who attended classes there were some of America's best scholars.

Space was at a premium in the two-hundred-year-old city. Homes and businesses stood wall to wall. Horses' hooves clopped noisily over cobblestone streets. Merchants in the nearby marketplace filled the early morning air with their calls. On warm days, the smell of the sea permeated the streets surrounding the wharves.

Sarah and William adjusted well to city life. They made new friends and kept busy with work, school and community activities. When she turned 43, Sarah even posed for a portrait. The famous artist, James Reid Lamblin, painted the lady editress. Today the portrait belongs to the Richards Free Library in Sarah's hometown of Newport.

Ladies Magazine continued to thrive. Both men and women writers contributed stories and articles to the periodical. Sarah's job involved not only editing other people's work, but also writing some of the pieces herself. She wrote poems, book reviews, articles, and editorials. And she did not only write for *Ladies Magazine*. She continued to write her own books as well as poems that appeared in popular collections.

Sarah published a small anthology of verse called *Poems for Our Children*. It included a poem that continues to be popular today:

MARY'S LAMB
Mary had a little lamb,
Its fleece was white as snow
And everywhere that Mary went
The lamb was sure to go...

Each poem in this little book taught a lesson of some kind. The last verse of Mary's Lamb is not often recited anymore. Today's children prefer the humor found in the beginning of the verse. The story tells of Mary's lamb following her to school. The children stop their work when the lamb enters their classroom:

He followed her to school one day
That was against the rule
It made the children laugh and play
To see a lamb at school,

But this, like the rest of Sarah's poems ends with a lesson. The moral is about loyalty, gentleness, and caring:

> And so the teacher turned him out,
> But still he lingered near
> And waited patiently about,
> Till Mary did appear…
>
> Why does the lamb love Mary so?
> The eager children cry,
> 'O Mary loved the lamb, you know,'
> The teacher did reply;—
>
> 'And you each gentle animal
> In confidence may bind,
> And make them follow at your call,
> If you are only *kind*.'

"Mary Had a Little Lamb" as it first appeared in Lowell Mason's Juvenile Lyre *in 1831. Today's children sing the poem to a different tune.*

Stories today do not usually contain such obvious moral lessons. Books written for children in the 1800s were written specifically to teach children how they should behave. In her introduction to *Poems for Our Children,* Sarah wrote:

> "…I know children love to read rhymes, and sing little verses; but they often read silly rhymes and such manner of spending their time is not good. I intended, when I began to write this book, to furnish you with a few pretty songs and poems which would teach you truths, and, I hope, induce you to love truth and goodness…"

Sarah believed children's play was part of learning. Students could feel successful while having fun.

Composer Lowell Mason was president of Boston's Handel and Haydn Society. He soon would become America's first public school music teacher. Mason wrote music for "Mary's Lamb" and some of Sarah's other poems. He included the songs in a book with the long title, *Juvenile Lyre: Or Hymns and Songs, Religious, Moral, and Cheerful, Set to Appropriate Music for the use of Primary and Common Schools.*

Teachers used the little songs in their classrooms. By 1832, children all over the country were singing "Mary's Lamb" as well as some of Sarah's other poems. They included "My Country," "Birds," and "Prayer."

By 1833, Sarah had been living in Boston for nearly five years. She had friends in the community. William was ten years old and more independent. Sarah felt comfortable using some of her free time to do good works. She was impressed by the ministry of a local preacher. Father Edward Taylor worked for the spiritual benefit of Boston's sailors. His chapel, called the Bethel, was well known. Father Taylor's wife worked by his side ministering to the families the sailors left behind.

At last Sarah had found a way to help people like her late brother, Charles. She and other Boston women offered to assist Mrs. Taylor. Together they founded the Seamen's Aid Society in 1833. Sarah was named president. At first, the women helped by sewing clothing for the poor families but they knew this was only a short-term solution. The sailor's families needed more than a handout. They needed ways to help themselves.

The group devised a plan: they would open their own store and sell sailor's clothing. The seamen's wives and daughters would make the clothing. The women

could earn a fair price for their work while the clothing would be sold at a cheaper price than clothes made in the "slop shops."

The Society planned classes to teach the young ladies how to sew, read, and write. They began a lending library. The Aid Society hoped that these methods would improve the lives of sailors' families.

Sarah spread the word about their plan to others interested in charitable works. In 1833, she wrote to Philadelphia activist and writer Matthew Carey:

> "...The Reverend Mr. Taylor is much impressed with...your views relative to the low rate of wages paid to females... The wages paid for hired help in families is probably as high as it ought to be—and there is demand for such help beyond the supply in our city—but poor women who have children or who are in ill health cannot go to work. They depend on the slop shops for much of their employment; and the prices paid for needle work at those places is to the utmost point reduced. Now, an establishment which would furnish work to those women

at fair and competent prices is all that is needed to remedy this evil. The slop shops would be obliged to raise their rate of prices, and then the seamstresses might live comfortably…"

Sarah went on to say that the idea for giving the women work rather than charity would be discussed at the next meeting of the Seamen's Aid Society in December.

During this same period, Sarah and John Blake had a new concern. For a while, *Ladies Magazine* had been unique. But a new periodical for women, started by Philadelphia publisher Louis Godey in 1830, was threatening the position of *Ladies Magazine. Godey's Lady's Book* was becoming very popular.

The first year's issues of *Godey's Lady's Book* had been somewhat dull and unimaginative. They included a few black and white illustrations and reprints of stories from other magazines. But Louis Godey was a determined businessman. By the second year he had improved *Lady's Book*. He began to compete seriously with *Ladies Magazine.* He kept a close eye on any new features introduced by Sarah Hale and John Blake. For example, only two months after *Ladies Magazine* had

Louis A. Godey, Prince of Publishers
From Godey's Lady's Book, *February, 1850*

done so, *Godey's Lady's Book* began to include colored fashion plates. Godey wanted "the Book" as he called it, to be the best. It could be the best, he decided, if he could merge with *Ladies Magazine.* He approached John Blake with the idea of combining the two publications.

At first, John Blake intended to keep his magazine independent. He had no desire to join Louis Godey. Sarah was relieved. For now, her job was safe. She continued to use *Ladies Magazine* to educate women and support important causes. As always, Sarah focused on education. She introduced the public to a different kind of school: the Boston School for the Blind, later called the Perkins Institute.

> "…We saw at (Dr. Howe's) school two little girls, sisters, of the ages eight and six… (In three months) they had learned to read correctly in the books prepared for the blind, and could perform sums in the simple rules of arithmetic and their knowledge of geography was wonderful. We came away fully impressed with the importance of educating the blind… and enabling them to get their own livelihood."

Later, such famous students as Laura Bridgman, Annie Sullivan, and Helen Keller would attend Perkins Institute.

Sarah's interest in all kinds of education extended beyond the borders of the United States. Greece won

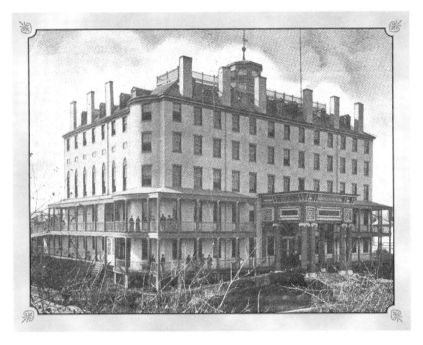

Sarah Hale's interest in education extended to such special institutions as the Boston School for the Blind led by Samuel G. Howe. The school is now over 175 years old and continues in Boston as the Perkins School for the Blind.

its independence from the Ottoman Empire and the Treaty of Constantinople was signed in 1832. Emma Willard wrote to Sarah requesting donations to start a school for girls in the war-ravaged country. The magazine's Boston readers organized a fair. It was held at Fanueil Hall—a large stone building nicknamed the "Cradle of Liberty" because of its importance during the American Revolution.

Over $2500 was raised for Mrs. Willard's new school. Sarah was pleased with what the ladies had accomplished. "Fanueil Hall," she wrote, "has increased in importance… (from the) Cradle of Liberty (to the) Temple of Charity." The fair's success would inspire Sarah at a later date.

During this period, Sarah's own children continued to follow their parents' ideals about hard work and education. Some of the Hale children were entering new periods in their lives. Sarah's eldest son, David, completed his studies at West Point. Even though he'd been one of the youngest members of his class, David was admired for his friendliness and intelligence. On July 1, 1833, he graduated 13th out of forty-three graduates of West Point. He became a Second Lieutenant in the artillery.

Horatio, Sarah's second son, came to Boston and entered Harvard College to study linguistics. He would learn how languages were formed. Like his mother, Horatio loved reading and writing and often wrote poetry.

The girls continued their studies at Emma Willard's School in Troy, New York.

Sarah missed her children. The family was often separated for long periods of time. In June, 1834, she wrote again to Matthew Carey. He had expected an article of his to appear in the May issue of *Ladies Magazine.* Sarah apologized that the piece had been delayed:

> "...I was preparing to visit my children who were at school in the country and whom I had not seen for six months—I rushed to get out the number for May...I ...lay your article aside intending I would provide the engravings to insert it in the June number..."

That same year, Boston citizens heard some good news. The Mechanics Association gave twenty-thousand dollars to the Bunker Hill Monument fund.

The amount was combined with the three thousand dollars Sarah's Committee of Correspondence had raised. An additional forty feet was added to the monument. Sarah was pleased with the progress but she longed to find a way to complete the project. Local newspapers reported that it was possible that the current generation would not live to see the finished monument.

Later in 1834, the *Ladies Magazine* changed its name to *American Ladies Magazine* because, Sarah wrote, "…we found there was a British periodical called '*The Ladies Magazine.*' We wished to have ours distinguished at once as American…"

Sarah became even more involved in *American Ladies Magazine* that year. At age forty-six, she became a part owner. It was one time that Sarah seemed to have made a poor decision. The United States was in the midst of an economic depression. People were out of work. There were fewer dollars for frills like magazines. Subscriptions began to fall. *American Ladies Magazine* was losing money.

Chapter Seven

Changes for Mrs. Hale
1835 – 1838

Sarah had edited her magazine for seven years. Her life was firmly entrenched in Boston. She had become a respected figure in the city. Her work with the Seamen's Aid Society was recognized not only in Boston but other port cities. The "lady editress"—as she called herself—had made many friends and influential contacts. But none of them could provide a magical solution to America's economy. None of them could save *American Ladies Magazine*. She and John Blake had to decide how to keep their magazine alive. Sarah still needed the income it provided to support herself and her younger children.

Sarah did not believe it was useful to fret. It was far better to work hard and try to fix problems. By 1835 all of her children were grown. William followed his brother Horatio into Harvard College. Sarah had more time to devote to her writing and editing.

Although she was part-owner of *American Ladies Magazine*, she continued to write her own books and produce other projects. These works included a popular collection of her essays and short stories called *Traits of American Life*. Sarah negotiated her own contracts with her publishers. She always asked for fair payment including ten percent in royalties and one free copy of the book for herself and each of her children. Today writers usually receive several free copies of their newly published books. Some historians believe Sarah Hale may have been one of the first writers to request this addition to her contract.

After the Ladies Fair had raised funds for Emma Willard's school in Greece, Sarah heard grumblings in the community about whether such fairs were appropriate. Some people believed that the young women who made, donated, and sold articles at the fair should not be involved in such a public display. Others believed that the wealthy were taking work from the poor by selling items made by the rich. Sarah addressed both issues in her new book:

> "...(men and women) are permitted to mingle together in elegant amusements, in the pursuits of literature, in the worship of God, we cannot discover any impropriety in their occasionally meeting at the shrine of Charity..."

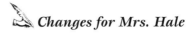

Sarah also believed that the poor benefited from the sale of new items created for the fairs. The items became popular and shops needed workers to keep up with the demand. Sarah felt that providing honest work for the poor was much more beneficial than merely giving charity:

> "...Giving alms to those who are able to work is a very bad plan...But we think the articles sold at the Fairs have increased the demand for fancy works of a similar description...Whatever is fashionable is soon necessary; and ...such articles have been sold at the Ladies' Fairs are now kept at many fancy shops...the ingenious and industrious poor are reaping benefits from this trade..."

Sarah encouraged the members of the Seamen's Aid Society to focus their work in the same direction. In 1836 the Society was ready to open its first store. Some of the sailors' wives were put in charge of running the store. Other wives and daughters sewed the clothing. They made the clothing for less money than the slop shops, sold it for less, and still made a profit. Slop shop owners were furious because the Society's store was a success.

The Seamen's Aid Society next opened a boarding house and a trade school for girls. The boarding house, called Mariner's House, was the first of many similar houses that would be built along the United States seacoast. It gave visiting sailors a place to stay, eat, and worship.

The girls attending the trade school were taught to sew and invited to borrow books from the school's lending library. The lending library itself was unusual. Even the famous Boston Public Library would not be founded for ten more years. At this time, few free public libraries existed. Most public libraries operated on a "subscription" method. Members paid a small fee to belong. For the poor, any fee was often more than they could afford.

While Boston's Seamen's Aid Society made progress, the news was not as good in other parts of the United States. The country continued to experience a financial depression. Some of the magazine's subscribers asked for extensions on their bills. Sarah often was forced to remind customers that they must pay for their subscriptions to *American Ladies Magazine:*

"Those of our subscribers who have promised to remit... (payment) in the Fall, will please observe their promise for never was the hour of peril near when remittances were more wanted."

The magazine continued to lose money. It may be for this reason that John Blake decided to accept Louis Godey's offer and sell his shares in the magazine. For months Godey had been writing articles praising Sarah Hale, her books, and her magazine. He was determined to get the attention of the lady editor! He was convinced that her talents could help to improve "the Book."

His tactics worked because following the sale of *American Ladies Magazine,* Sarah agreed to become editor of Philadelphia's *Godey's Lady's Book.* Just as before, Sarah accepted the job on condition that she did not have to move immediately. Horatio would be graduating from Harvard in a few months, but William still had several years of classes to complete. Sarah did not intend to leave Boston until William graduated.

She was forty-nine years old when she began her new job in January, 1837. The first magazine she edited for Louis Godey was a combined issue of both the *Lady's Book* and *American Ladies*. Godey said the union of the two magazines was "like two pleasant voices blended into one sweet melody."

Louis Godey allowed Sarah to edit the magazine in any way she saw fit. There was only one exception: "the Book" must not take any political sides.

This rule did not keep Sarah from writing about social issues that she felt needed correcting. A favorite topic for her editorials was the need to pass laws about property rights for women. Most states had laws that said when a woman married, anything she owned became her husband's property. Sarah fought for changes in these laws:

> "The barbarous custom of wresting
> from a woman whatever she possesses,
> whether by inheritance, donation, or her
> own industry…and conferring it…upon
> the man she marries, to be used at his
> discretion and will…without allowing
> her any control…(is) a monstrous
> perversion of justice by law…"

A woman's savings could be wasted by a foolish husband or used to pay his debts. The state of Louisiana already had passed a law allowing women control over their own money. The state of New York was trying to pass a similar law. "May their example...awaken the attention of the wise and good in other states of the Union," Sarah wrote.

Sarah had a personal interest in the passage of such a law. It might have helped her friend, Emma Willard. Mrs. Willard had been widowed for many years when she met Dr. Christopher Yates. Dr. Yates was always courteous in public. He courted Emma Willard for quite a while before asking her to marry him. Few people knew that Christopher Yates was looking for a rich wife. Emma Willard not only had a thriving girls' school, she had made quite a bit of money from the sale of her textbooks. Friends, who were fooled by Dr. Yates' charm, encouraged Emma to accept his proposal.

Emma must have had some misgivings about the marriage. She listened to her friends, but not before she carefully arranged things so that her son and his wife would take over her school. Trustees would handle most of her money and property. This seriously limited the amount of money Christopher Yates could get. It was a wise move. Doctor Yates, it turned out, had many gambling debts.

Emma's friendship with Sarah soured around this

time. Emma and Christopher Yates moved to Boston from New York. Dr. Yates' true character was soon revealed. Emma's marriage was almost immediately an unhappy one. She did something very unusual for that period. After only nine months of marriage, she left her husband. She fled Boston and went to live with a sister in Connecticut.

Some historians claim Sarah tried to bring Emma and Dr. Yates back together. She may not have been aware of the problems Emma had faced with him. Emma was angered by the interference.

Sarah soon learned that Dr. Yates had a side he did not show in public. After Emma left him, Yates had terrible, insulting articles printed about Emma and her school in a New York newspaper.

Sarah may have wondered how the new laws she worked for could have saved her friendship with Emma. Without the possibility that Dr. Yates could get his hands on Emma Willard's money, he might never have tried to become part of her life and Sarah might not have lost such an admired friend.

Chapter Eight
Another Great Loss
1839 – 1841

Sarah was hurt by Emma Willard's reaction but she did not stop supporting Emma's work in education. She continued to praise the Troy Female Seminary and print favorable reviews of Emma's books. She hoped to reconcile with her friend.

For Sarah, the next few years were another period of great change. Not only had she become editor of a different magazine, but she soon would have to leave another home.

Godey's Lady's Book and *American Ladies Magazine* were successfully merged. Louis Godey had been true to his word and given Sarah nearly free rein to improve "the Book." Sarah and Godey were a good team. They planned to develop a magazine that would appeal to readers all over the United States and its territories.

Sarah and Mr. Godey tried new features while hanging on to successful ones. "The Book" continued the practice of including fashion plates. Sarah still disapproved of most of the styles, but there was one thing about the plates she did like. They were hand-painted. The painting was done by women in their homes. Sarah understood the importance of this kind of work for women like herself. It was the sort of work that could be done while a woman cared for her children. There was a slight problem with this idea, however. The fashion plates were supposed to be painted a certain way. The women painters were told which colors to add to each dress design. Sometimes a painter ran out of the required color. Rather than lose a day's work, the painter often substituted a different color. Neighbors comparing their issues of "the Book" might find that one magazine featured a plate showing a yellow dress while the other would have the same dress in blue.

Louis Godey did not want to admit this was unplanned. He told readers this was another service of "the Book."

> "We now colour our plates to different patterns so that two persons in a place may compare their fashions and adopt those colours that they suppose may be most suitable to their figures and complexions."

The wily publisher knew how to turn a problem into a solution!

Godey's Lady's Book was popular with writers as well as readers. Sarah and Mr. Godey let it be known that they did not believe in the methods used by most magazines of the time.

It was the custom for newspapers and magazines to steal articles and stories from each other. This practice was called pirating. While the authors might get credit for their work, they were not paid for the use of the reprinted pieces. Authors certainly didn't like to see their work reprinted for free. Sarah remembered how important it was for her to get paid for her writing after David's death. A magazine like *Godey's* might pay an author a good sum of money for an original story only to see it reprinted in a newspaper before the magazine had been delivered to its farthest customers. If this happened too often readers would be angry. No one wanted to pay for a magazine that contained only old stories and articles.

Louis Godey and Sarah proceeded to copyright "the Book." To copyright an artist or writer's work means to own the only legal right to produce or publish the work. This wasn't a new idea. A law had been passed in the 1700s allowing writers and editors to protect their work. Sarah and Louis used the law to make it illegal for anyone to reprint stories from *Godey's Lady's Book* without permission. Publishers who wished to reprint stories or articles would have to pay for them. As a result, "the Book" was able to feature many important writers of the period including Harriet Beecher Stowe, Edgar Alan Poe, Horace Greeley, and Mrs. Lydia H. Sigourney.

Many publishers were furious! They thought Louis Godey was turning his back on the rest of the publishing community. These business owners depended on getting good stories for free. Pirating helped to keep their costs down.

Sarah and Mr. Godey wanted to guarantee their readers fresh stories from the best writers. Many of the stories and poems were labeled "Written for the *Lady's Book.*" They also promised to pay top prices for well-written pieces. But Sarah didn't want writers to think that she would accept poor quality work. Sarah wrote hundreds of words every day. She knew how important it was to revise one's writing. She told young writers that if they wanted to be original, they should also be concise: "To poets, whether young or old, the advice of Dryden is invaluable...

'A hundred times consider what you've said,
Polish, re-polish, every colour lay,
And sometimes add, but oftener take away.'"

Within a year of Sarah becoming editor, *Godey's Lady's Book* became one of the most popular magazines in America. Sarah had many reasons to be optimistic about its success. But 1839 would prove to be a very difficult year. Early in that year, Sarah's oldest son, David, was sent to guard the border of Canada. The young lieutenant had spent several years in Florida fighting in the Seminole Wars. Sarah was concerned about David going from a very warm climate to a much colder one. She wondered if he would be able to withstand the change. But David was a soldier. A soldier must obey orders and go where he is sent. Sarah's fears became a reality when twenty-five-year-old David died of pneumonia in April, 1839. This was the hardest thing she had faced since the death of her husband. She wrote to Louis Godey:

> "It is not a common loss that I mourn. My son was so noble...I depended on him as a friend who would never disappoint me, and as the protector of my daughters and young son...His death has destroyed all my plans of life..."

Sarah became depressed and was unable to handle

the demands of her job. By December, 1839, Louis Godey appointed Lydia Sigourney to assist with the editorial duties of "the Book." It was never Godey's intention to replace Sarah, however, and he made that very clear to his readers. He understood that she needed time to mourn. Subscribers understood, too. Many sent letters and "the Book" printed poems readers had written and dedicated to David's memory.

Within a year of David's death, Sarah began, once again, to take a more active role in the work of editing "the Book." She prepared, also, for William's last year at Harvard. Soon it would be time for her to leave Boston and move to Philadelphia.

In 1840, her final year in Boston, Sarah continued to work with the Seamen's Aid Society and do other good works. She learned that the Bunker Hill Monument was once again at a standstill. No more money was being donated or pledged. Sarah decided she could not ask women to again merely donate money. She determined that it was time for the ladies to try a different method of raising the needed funds. Sarah proposed another "Women's Fair." Money may have been in the hands of the men but many other things were part of women's domain. Sarah asked women all over the country to

Faneuil Hall was again the chosen site for the Women's Fair.
The amount raised by the ladies was enough to complete the
Bunker Hill Monument.

donate hand-made crafts that could be sold to benefit the completion of the Bunker Hill Monument. The ladies began to knit, sew, and preserve home-grown foods. Donations came from nearly every state and territory.

"The Fair" was held once again at Fanueil Hall near the Boston wharves. It lasted for seven days. People came from miles to see and buy the hand-made items. In the end, more than thirty thousand dollars were raised—enough to complete the monument!

It was a great moment not only for Sarah and the Monument Association, but also for American women. This fair had shown that women were just as capable as men when it came to organizing and carrying out a plan to its successful end. Many people believed that the fair also changed attitudes about women becoming partners in charitable organizations. Until then, men had run most of these groups. Now, more women's auxiliaries were formed to help with charity work.

After all her support for the Bunker Hill Monument, Sarah was not in Boston to see the completed structure. Additions were still being made to the obelisk when William graduated from Harvard in 1841. Sarah prepared to leave Boston and move to the publishing capital of the United States: Philadelphia.

Chapter Nine

Philadelphia
1841 – 1846

Sarah was 54 years old and, for a third time, starting a new life.

All of Sarah's children were now adults. William followed his brother Horatio's example and did very well at Harvard. He graduated second in his class. Within the year, he moved to Virginia to study law.

Horatio worked as a linguist. He went to the Oregon Territory as part of the first United States Exploring Expedition sent out by Congress. He studied and documented Native American languages. Sarah did not often hear from her second son and she worried about his well-being. She wrote to Eliza Leslie, a friend and writer who often contributed to *Godey's Lady's Book*:

> "...I have not, for four months, had any letter from my son (Horatio) but the last news from the Exploring Expedition represented all in good health. I feel very anxious to hear that the vessels have safely returned from their southern exploration—..."

Horatio did return safely and went on to study law.

Josepha and Frances had both graduated from

Emma Willard's Troy Female Seminary. Josepha had become a teacher. She taught for many years in the South. She moved to Philadelphia and opened her own school for young women. Frances Ann had also studied to be a teacher and had taught at Emma Willard's school for a while. Shortly after Sarah's move to Philadelphia, Frances Ann married Dr. Lewis Hunter. They too, would live in Philadelphia. Sarah would not be alone in her new city.

Now that her youngest child had chosen his career, Sarah felt free to leave her beloved Boston. She was sad to go but was beginning to find the cold New England winters hard on her health. Philadelphia's climate would be slightly milder.

Her move benefited *Godey's Lady's Book,* too. Since Sarah had become editor, she and Louis Godey had had to worry about the mail delivering her writings and editorials safely from Boston to Philadelphia. Magazines were expected to publish each month and on time. When Sarah reached Philadelphia, the lady editor and her publisher boss would no longer be at the mercy of the weather and the postal delivery.

"The Book" continued to be innovative. Sarah

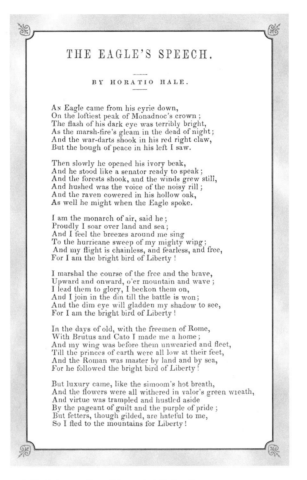

THE EAGLE'S SPEECH.

BY HORATIO HALE.

An Eagle came from his eyrie down,
On the loftiest peak of Monadnoc's crown ;
The flash of his dark eye was terribly bright,
As the marsh-fire's gleam in the dead of night ;
And the war-darts shook in his red right claw,
But the bough of peace in his left I saw.

Then slowly he opened his ivory beak,
And he stood like a senator ready to speak ;
And the forests shook, and the winds grew still,
And hushed was the voice of the noisy rill ;
And the raven cowered in his hollow oak,
As well he might when the Eagle spoke.

I am the monarch of air, said he ;
Proudly I soar over land and sea ;
And I feel the breezes around me sing
To the hurricane sweep of my mighty wing ;
And my flight is chainless, and fearless, and free,
For I am the bright bird of Liberty !

I marshal the course of the free and the brave,
Upward and onward, o'er mountain and wave ;
I lead them to glory, I beckon them on,
And I join in the din till the battle is won ;
And the dim eye will gladden my shadow to see,
For I am the bright bird of Liberty !

In the days of old, with the freemen of Rome,
With Brutus and Cato I made me a home ;
And my wing was before them unwearied and fleet,
Till the princes of earth were all low at their feet,
And the Roman was master by land and by sea,
For he followed the bright bird of Liberty !

But luxury came, like the simoom's hot breath,
And the flowers were all withered in valor's green wreath,
And virtue was trampled and hustled aside
By the pageant of guilt and the purple of pride ;
But fetters, though gilded, are hateful to me,
So I fled to the mountains for Liberty !

Like his mother, Horatio Hale also wrote poetry.
This poem was published in a collection of writings
about New Hampshire. It appeared in 1844
when Horatio was twenty-seven.

pointed out in her editorial of January, 1841 that this first edition of the new year was "...entirely composed of contributions from female writers." No other magazine had ever claimed that distinction.

That year, Sarah renewed her friendship with the writer Edgar Allan Poe. Poe also lived in Philadelphia. He had attended West Point briefly at the same time as David Hale. By 1841 he already was well-known for his eerie stories and poems. Poe recently had been hired as the new editor of a rival magazine: *Graham's Lady's and Gentleman's Magazine.* Making Poe editor was a smart move on the part of publisher George Graham. Poe was a popular writer. His involvement with *Graham's* practically guaranteed the magazine's subscriptions would increase. This situation didn't please Louis Godey, of course.

George Graham aimed his magazine at men *and* women. He included a balance of articles as well as the popular fashion plates. His plates showed three to four new styles as opposed to the two "the Book" usually featured. Within months Sarah and Godey made several changes in their "Book" to keep pace with *Graham's.*

Today we read reviews of television shows or films in the newspaper. Newspapers in Sarah's time often

By 1841, Graham's Magazine *was in fierce competition with* Godey's Lady's Book. *This fashion plate appeared in the October 1841 edition and featured four designs. Until that year,* Godey's *plates usually showed only two designs.*

reviewed magazines such as *Godey's* and *Graham's*. The changes Sarah and Mr. Godey made were well-received. In August, 1841, Louis Godey wrote:

> "We feel thankful to our brethren of the press for their kindly notice of the improvements of this volume. We have been over Twelve Years publishing the Lady's Book and we promise our subscribers that we will not be surpassed by any other publication..."

Colored plates in *Godey's Lady's Book* now pictured four to six new fashions for women and children. The print was larger, clearer, and easier to read. Ornate borders decorated each page. Sarah reminded readers and contributing authors that she would not reprint stories. "Our columns demand original contributions," she wrote.

Sarah and Mr. Godey made these changes not only to keep readers from switching to *Graham's*. They also hoped their readers would like the new format so much that they wouldn't mind that *Godey's Lady's Book* was nearly 200 pages shorter than the previous year's volume. Hard times had befallen the publishing world in 1842. By November, Sarah was once again

reminding subscribers to pay their bills.

That month, Sarah began to suggest a new idea: a national day of Thanksgiving. Many states and territories set aside one day during the year as a day of thanksgiving. These special events were usually harvest festivals held in the fall but the dates varied all over the country.

Sarah reminded her readers that when George Washington was president he issued a proclamation making the fourth Thursday in November a national day of Thanksgiving. A proclamation is not a law, however. It is only a suggestion. After Washington's death the country-wide holiday was forgotten. The states returned to their individual celebrations.

The New England states, where the Pilgrims had settled, had a long tradition of celebrating Thanksgiving each year. Sarah had even included a description of a New England Thanksgiving in her first novel, *Northwood*. The Romilly family, like others in their town, prepared a bountiful meal:

> "...every farmer in the country being, at this season of the year plentifully supplied, and everyone proud of displaying his abundance and prosperity..."

The family feasted not only on turkey but goose, duckling, and a large chicken pie. Plates of pickles, preserves, and butter took up any bit of space left on the table. The family shared plum pudding, custard, and pies for dessert. A large pumpkin pie was set in the center of the sideboard. It was this kind of Thanksgiving that Sarah Hale believed every American should share.

But Sarah had another reason for urging the entire country to set aside the same day to celebrate Thanksgiving. The same issues plagued the United States since *Northwood* originally had been published. Politics were full of heated discussions about slavery and states' rights. Many Americans felt that the states were closer to war because of their differences.

Sarah saw the celebration of a national Thanksgiving as a way to remind both the north and south of its common beginnings. She not only wrote an editorial, but sent letters to the governors of each state and territory, congressmen, and even President John Tyler. Several states decided to hold their celebrations on the date suggested by Sarah, but President Tyler did not respond. Sarah was disappointed but felt strongly that her idea was a good one and worth trying again.

In 1842 Sarah also honored her old friend, Emma Willard. The December Editor's Book Table contained a glowing review of Mrs. Willard's latest book, *History of the United States*. Sarah recommended it not only as a wonderful textbook but as a "valuable addition to our family libraries and national literature." Sarah would not let the lapse in their friendship keep her from supporting the cause of women's education.

In 1844, when Sarah was 56 years old, her daughter Frances Ann and Doctor Hunter were married. Soon after, the Hunters invited Sarah to live with them. Their house on Locust Street would be Sarah's final home. She moved into a spacious room that contained a sleeping area, a sofa for visitors, and of course, a large table for writing.

During the next few years "the Book" took even more risks. Sarah began to promote several ideas that some people found unusual and even shocking!

Miss Eliza Leslie, a regular contributor to *Godey's Lady's Book* was hired by the magazine to take a train trip from Philadelphia to Niagara Falls. She would travel without a father, brother, or other male relative to help her. Some people found the idea of women traveling alone difficult to accept, but transportation

The Bunker Hill Monument was finished after Sarah Hale moved to Philadelphia. Daniel Webster was the featured speaker at the celebration held in 1843. He said, "The last effort, and the last contribution, were from a different source... The mothers and daughters of the land contributed thus, most successfully..."

in the United States had improved since the American Revolution. Canals had been built all over the country. Steamships traveled up and down America's larger rivers. The railroad was becoming a popular way to travel. Better transportation allowed people to travel farther than before. Miss Leslie wrote a column for "the Book" showing how easily women could travel through the country.

By 1846, the western part of the United States was opening up to new settlement. People were flocking to the western territories to buy cheap land and build their own homes away from the crowded cities. *Godey's Lady's Book* supported the idea of Western Expansion.

Although Sarah could not write about the politics involved in the settlement of the west, she and Louis Godey found other ways to encourage America's pioneers. "The Book" introduced a new department: "Godey's Model Cottage" complete with illustrations and descriptions of the house's design. Western settlers could bring the house plans with them to build when they established new towns. Sarah wrote frequently about western development and encouraged bold readers to try pioneer life.

Sarah promoted other opinions, too. She wrote many articles urging that women be hired as teachers for younger children. They should not only teach preschoolers in dame schools as she had done. They should be put in charge of the primary grades. Women, Sarah said, had the natural patience necessary for dealing with younger children. The magazine became the official promoter of the Ladies Education Society. The society raised money to train women teachers. These young ladies were then sent to open schools in the pioneer towns.

For years, *Godey's Lady's Book* had included sheet music for readers to learn and play in their homes. Now "the Book" encouraged people to take up dancing and introduced music for a new dance: the polka! At that time, some people felt it wasn't decent for men and women to dance with their arms around each other. Sarah pointed out that not only could dancing be fun, it was great exercise!

The world was changing, but along with progress came new problems. Sarah was ready to pick up her pen and address these issues.

Chapter Ten

The Sweep of Our Eagle's Wing
1847 – 1860

American society had changed dramatically since the day Sarah Hale was left alone to care for her five young children. Since that time, her life had been filled with risks.

When she left New Hampshire, Sarah took a risk by accepting a job no other woman in America had ever done. She faced the disapproval of many people who believed that a woman had a certain place in society and should concern herself mostly with her family.

She took risks by writing about sensitive topics: female education and property rights for women. Sarah also promoted the idea of training women as doctors. She urged society to change its opinions on fashion, child care for working mothers, and methods of charity.

As 1847 began, Sarah continued to walk a fine line in her writings in order to make her points while obeying Louis Godey's rules about keeping "the Book" out of politics.

During the middle years of the 1800s, Sarah saw many of her causes become realities. The articles and essays she wrote at that time celebrated the changes that were occurring in the United States.

She rejoiced when Elizabeth Blackwell became the first woman to graduate from the Geneva Medical School in 1848. Her graduation provided the impetus for other schools to take action. Harvard Medical School and other colleges soon began to accept women students.

In 1848 gold was discovered in California at Sutter's Mill. By the next year thousands of people were heading to the West Coast to try and make their fortunes. Some people tried their luck in the gold fields. Others brought food and materials to sell to the miners. Gold Rushers' tent "towns" sprang up throughout California. By April, 1849, Sarah reported that the Ladies Education Society had sent one hundred teachers to establish schools in these new California towns.

In 1850, *Godey's Lady's Book* celebrated its twentieth anniversary. Sarah could see the impact her writings had had on the public, but while she had strong attitudes about women's roles in society, there were some changes Sarah would not support.

For two years, Elizabeth Cady Stanton and others had been asking Congress to give women the right to vote. Any free, white man could vote—whether he was educated or not—but a well-informed, intelligent woman could not participate in the country's elections.

(Remember that slavery still existed in the United States at this time. Only a few northeastern states allowed free black men to vote).

Surprisingly, Sarah did not agree that women should vote. She felt politics were vulgar and unfeminine. She couldn't use "the Book" to discuss this issue directly. Instead, she continued to write about the rights women had already won. Even without the vote, Sarah believed women could influence the way the country behaved and thought.

During this period, the United States continued to face serious divisions. The issues of slavery and states' rights were the constant political topics. Congress ironed out the Compromise of 1850. This series of acts provided stronger fugitive slave laws to appease the south while bringing in California as a free state to calm the abolitionists. Sarah had her own strong opinions about these matters. During the next decade, both her personal and magazine writings focused on causes that shared a common theme: national unity.

Some of Sarah's opinions can be read in a collection of quotations she edited and published in 1850, *A Complete Dictionary of Poetical Quotations (Comprising the Most Excellent and Appropriate Passages in the Old*

British Poets; with Choice and Copious Selections from the Best Modern British and American Poets).

The project had been started by an Englishman living in Philadelphia, John F. Addington. He never completed the book. Sarah added modern poets to the project. She included some of her own work as well as the work of some of her friends such as Oliver Wendell Holmes and Lydia Sigourney.

The possibility of a civil war continued to threaten the United States. Some of the quotations selected by Sarah may have allowed her to express the feelings and opinions she had to keep out of "the Book:"

> Ah! Why will kings forget that they are men?
> And men that they are brethren? Why delight
> In Human sacrifice? Why burst the ties
> Of nature, that should knit their souls together?
> > From *Porteus's Death*

One of Sarah's own poems expressed her true feelings:

> O, war is cruel-hearted! ay, the man
> That in the private walks of life was kind,...
> Why he, when war's stern strength is on his soul,
> Will stalk in apathy o'er slaughter'd friends...
> > From Mrs. Hale's *Ormond Grovesnor*

In the *Lady's Book* Sarah urged mothers to teach their children to be patriotic. She chose her words carefully. She knew that the citizens of each state often behaved as if their state were a separate country. This kind of thinking could only lead to more division.

> "...begin early, with your little ones, American mother and teach them of America... Do not confine their young hearts to the boundaries of any single state. Let their patriot love go out wide as the sweep of our eagle's wing...:

In March, 1852, one of the writers who had sometimes contributed to *Godey's Lady's Book*, Harriet Beecher Stowe, published a remarkable novel: *Uncle Tom's Cabin*. The book tells about "Uncle Tom," a house slave who is sold by his first owners. His next owners are cruel. In the story, Uncle Tom dies at the hands of their heartless overseer, Simon Legree.

The book's impact was immediate. Northern abolitionists declared the novel was a true picture of slavery. Southern slave owners said the story was slanted. It was just another attempt to destroy a way of life northerners did not understand. Mrs. Stowe's book added fuel to the nation's growing arguments. The whispers about the possibility of civil war were turning into demands for secession.

Friends urged Sarah to allow a fifth printing of her popular novel, *Northwood.* Worried about the fate of her beloved country, Sarah agreed. In the introduction she reminded readers of "…those great men, 'Defenders of the Constitution,' who 'know no North and no South,' but wherever the …Eagle and the Stars keep guard is their country…" Sarah hoped that *Northwood*, with its descriptions of a more peaceful America, would help calm the anger inflamed by *Uncle Tom's Cabin.*

Sarah also wrote a new novel that more clearly expressed her own prejudices about slavery. Her attitudes echoed those of many other Americans living at that time. Sarah believed slavery was wrong but she also believed people of the black race should be returned to Africa. In her mind, Africa was their true home. Sarah failed to see that, by 1852, the United States *was* home to the majority of its black community. They had been born in the United States and knew as little about life in Africa as any other native-born Americans.

Sarah based the plot of her new novel on an earlier social experiment. In 1820, a group of white Americans had raised funds to purchase land on the western coast of Africa. Their goal was to establish a colony of freed American slaves. They called the new colony "Liberia" from the Latin term for freedom or liberty.

Sarah used these events as the backdrop for *Liberia: or, Mr. Peyton's Experiments.* She believed that if slave owners followed the plan her fictional characters did of sending slaves back to Africa, a peaceful compromise could be reached between the arguing states.

Sarah tried other ways to encourage the states to work together while maintaining Louis Godey's rule about staying out of politics. She continued, for example, to suggest the states unite through the celebration of a national Thanksgiving holiday. By the fall of 1852, all the United States territories and all but two states had set aside the fourth Thursday in November as a day of national Thanksgiving. Sarah wrote letters each year asking the current president and the Congress to make this celebration law. No one in the federal government responded to her repeated requests.

Sarah called attention to another cause that would require cooperation between the states. In 1855 "the Book" joined forces with the *Southern Literary Journal.* The two magazines united to promote the work of the

Ladies Mount Vernon Association. Its purpose was to help raise funds to save Mount Vernon in Virginia. This farm had been George Washington's home. He and his wife, Martha, were buried on its grounds. The land and buildings at Mount Vernon were no longer used and were in disrepair. A descendant of General Washington owned the property. The Association wanted to buy Mount Vernon and turn it into a museum and shrine honoring the first president.

Sarah hoped that since the northern and southern *colonies* had been united under the leadership of the great general, perhaps the northern and southern *states* could work together again in his memory and save Washington's home. Sarah had another reason to help the Association. Her sister-in-law, also named Sarah, was one of its state leaders. By including articles about the Mount Vernon Association in the *Lady's Book*, Sarah could now return the help David's brother's wife had given so generously when she took in Josepha and Frances Ann while Sarah settled in Boston.

The project was an ambitious one. The Association wanted to guarantee that the farm would not go to another private owner. The current owner wanted a fair price for the property. He agreed to sell it for two hundred thousand dollars. The Mount Vernon Association planned fancy balls, plays, and talks by the famous orator Edward Everett as well as other events to help raise funds.

By 1857, nearly seventy-five thousand dollars had been raised or pledged. Sarah praised the efforts of all the participants and wrote:

> "...we hope that in this Association, the North and South will meet together, and the East and West unite, and all be as one in this work of love..."

None of Sarah's urgings could stop the inevitable, however. She prepared for a frightening future. When Florence Nightingale published a book on practical nursing in 1860, Sarah called it "...one of the most important works ever put forth by a woman..." She urged her readers to purchase a copy and learn all they could "...before it was needed." If the country could not stop its march towards a terrible war, then its citizens must be prepared for it.

The Mount Vernon Ladies Association took ownership of George Washington's farm in February, 1860. They had succeeded in preserving Washington's home but nothing, it seemed, could preserve the country from war.

Abraham Lincoln was elected President of the United States nine months later on November 6, 1860. Southern states were angered that an "abolitionist" had been chosen to lead the country. By the following month South Carolina officially seceded from the Union.

Chapter Eleven

The War Years
1861 – 1865

Six other states followed South Carolina's lead. By February 1861 the seven states had met, written a constitution, and formed a separate country: the Confederate States of America. They chose Jefferson Davis as their first president. They accomplished all of this before Abraham Lincoln took his own oath of office in March.

In April President Lincoln ordered supplies sent to Union troops at Fort Sumter in Charleston Harbor. Confederate soldiers attacked and the Union military was forced to surrender the fort. Lincoln saw that war could not be avoided. He called for volunteers. Young men in the North formed an army in blue, prepared to defend the Union. In response, young men in the South formed an army in gray, prepared to defend their homes and their way of life.

These were the most important events to have affected the United States since the Revolutionary War but they were never mentioned directly in "the Book." Louis Godey stuck to his rule that politics would not be part of his magazine. Sarah later wrote that *Godey's Lady's Book* was meant, during the national upheaval, to be a "lodge in the wilderness...

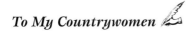
a quiet, cultured garden on which the burning lava had not even breathed…"

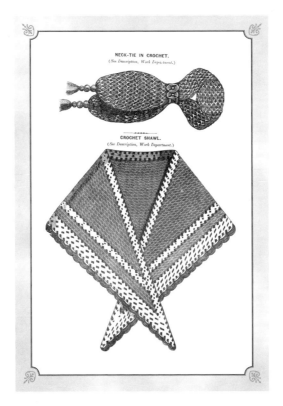

Godey's Lady's Book *did not refer directly to America's great Civil War. Instead, in the mid-1800s, the magazine included craft patterns and music as well as its usual artistic engravings and fashion plates.*

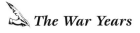

Sarah was 73 years old when the war began. Most women her age would be content to slow their pace and allow younger people to take over the majority of life's work, but Sarah's work habits had changed very little since she began her duties as editor.

The war seemed to fuel her ambition. Her beloved country was finally split in two. She could not direct her magazine's articles at the politics involved. Instead, Sarah focused on the soldiers and the families they had left behind.

Only two months after the start of the war, *Godey's* featured an article entitled "The Manufacture of Gunpowder" to give the reader "...a clear account of the various processes that are gone through to produce this important element of war..." Sarah published sentimental stories such as "The Soldier's Sister" and included military books in her reviews. She did not forget that her readers came from all the states and territories. She reviewed books written by both northern and southern authors even though "the Book" could not reach most of its southern readers while the war went on.

So many young men were gone to war. They left behind not only their families but their jobs. Sarah suggested that widows and single women be allowed to take over jobs normally thought of as "men's work." Why couldn't a woman become a postmistress or a clerk? She reminded readers "...a good handwriting, dexterity in accounts...are not beyond the powers of educated young women."

By 1863, the war had been raging for two long years. Time was beginning to take its toll on the lady editor. In the midst of the national struggle, Sarah faced another more personal tragedy.

Just a few blocks from her Locust Street home was the beautiful area known as Rittenhouse Square. Philadelphia's Boarding and Day School for Young Ladies was located at number 1826. The school was owned and run by Sarah's youngest daughter, Josepha.

On May 3, 1863 Josepha died suddenly at her desk. She was only forty-three years old. Josepha had become everything her mother had hoped: an educated, independent woman. Sarah wrote, "the mourning hearts she has left behind...feel...an irreparable loss..."

It was difficult for Sarah to have outlived yet another of her children. She stopped going to her office

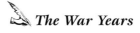

each day. She began to spend more and more time in her room, and, with the help of her grandson, Richard Hunter, did her editorial work and writing from home. It would have been another long, sad year but that November Sarah received news she long had been waiting for. For twenty years Sarah had written letters and editorial asking for a national day of Thanksgiving. One president after another had ignored Sarah's suggestions but Sarah did not give up.

She continued to suggest that the last Thursday in November would be the perfect time to celebrate. In her Editor's Table she again reminded readers that, by November, farm work was generally finished, elections were over, and summer travelers had returned home.

On September 28, 1863, Sarah addressed a letter to President Abraham Lincoln:

> "Permit me as editress of the 'Lady's Book' to request a few moments of your precious time while laying before you a subject of deep interest to myself and as I think even to the President of our Republic, of some importance. This object is to have the day of our annual Thanksgiving made a national and fixed Union Festival."

Sarah included letters from governors of various states who agreed to honor the date. She added copies of several of her editorials that marked the progress she had made with her campaign. She dared to make one other suggestion:

> "An immediate proclamation would be necessary so as to reach all the states in season for. . . appointment. . . by governors."

In the middle of the great Civil War, President Lincoln saw merit in Sarah's suggestion. By his word, all the states could be reunited—even if only for one day. Just five days after Sarah's letter was sent, President Abraham Lincoln proclaimed Thursday, November 26th, 1863, a day of National Thanksgiving. The proclamation was read in churches all over the country. It asked everyone to take a moment on that day to thank God for His blessings and pray "to heal the wounds of [our] nation."

Sarah wondered if she would ever get to see her idea become law. It would not happen during Abraham Lincoln's term of office. A year-and-a-half after that first proclamation, on April 15, 1865, Lincoln—the first president to act on Sarah's suggestion—died. He was killed by an assassin, John Wilkes Booth, just one

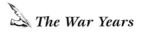

week after the end of the Civil War.

The Sunday following President Lincoln's death was Easter. For Christians it is the most sacred date on their calendars. Since the war was over, many Americans looked forward to this Easter as a time of special rejoicing. But on that Easter Sunday in 1865, churches all over America were draped in black "to mourn..." as Louis Godey wrote in a publisher's note, "a just man fallen."

In the four years of the Civil War thousands and thousands of men had died. *Godey's Lady's Book* included no editorials about the war. No mention was made of the Emancipation Proclamation. No articles were published about the terrible battles at Vicksburg and Gettysburg. The burning of Atlanta was never noted. Some historians believe that *Godey's Lady's Book* lost an opportunity to sway public opinion and help shorten the war. The magazine had great influence on American opinions.

Sarah and Mr. Godey never meant for their "Book" to do any more than offer solace to America's women. For the editor and publisher, the war's end would mean a return to normalcy. Their Southern readership would return.

Chapter Twelve

Towards a New Beginning
1866 – 1876

The Civil War changed American lives forever. After it ended, some families shared the relief of long-awaited homecomings. Others shared the misery of returning to homes destroyed by war. The Union had survived but few people felt victorious. Too many lives had been lost. The anger and hurt that exploded into war had to be abandoned. Emotions had to be channeled into Reconstruction.

Sarah understood what it meant to start over. She had done it many times in her life. She knew how to encourage her beloved America to begin a new life of its own.

While Sarah could not discuss her feelings about the war directly in the *Lady's Book,* it was easy to see where her heart was. The causes she supported before and during the war, the stories she chose for "the Book," showed her first loyalty was to the American family and second, to a united country. In Sarah's eyes, a strong country was made up of strong families. In the middle of the war, Sarah published a letter from "A Lady of Pennsylvania" in "the Book:"

> "The large armies which now have to be
> raised have taken men by the thousands

and thousands from their households, and it is feared, that among these brave soldiers many who have gone forth will only leave the record of their names as an inheritance to their bereaved families."

Perhaps Sarah herself was that "Lady of Pennsylvania." The letter certainly echoed the feelings Sarah experienced when her husband David died leaving his family with barely more than the "record of [his] name."

Now that the war was over, Sarah thought of those women and families who were left alone as she had been. It was time for "the Book" to help American women cope with their new challenges. Sarah was nearly eighty years old. She had already had a long and useful life but she continued to devote herself to several new causes.

Because of the war, thousands of women had become, like Sarah, the head of their households. Few had the advantages she did: a supportive family, the help of good friends, and the encouragement to become educated and self-reliant.

Sarah continued to use her power as editor of America's most popular women's magazine to try and make changes in people's attitudes and behaviors. The *Lady's Book* often included new suggestions for jobs that could be done by women. Sarah paid special attention to news from other countries concerning the different ways women earned their living across the sea. She wrote about women in Europe who used painting or fine beadwork to support their families.

Sarah also reminded her readers of the changes that had taken place in American attitudes from the time *Godey's Lady's Book* had first come into print. She pointed out that in the forty years since she had first begun to suggest it, one hundred thousand young women had become public school teachers. There were now almost twice as many women teachers as men.

As a child, Sarah had been surprised when she'd read *The Mysteries of Udolpho* because it had been written by a woman. Now, Sarah pointed out, "women write the great majority of children's books...religious and Sunday school books...They contribute largely to periodical literature."

Sarah was still brimming with ideas. She suggested that women could become telegraph operators. This type of work had barely existed even twenty years before. It required no physical strength, just a sturdy hand, good penmanship, and the ability to learn Morse code. Women also could work with architects to help design more efficient homes. Some women could earn their living in the arts.

She did not approve, however, of the great number of women and children who were forced by circumstances to work in the New England cloth factories. "It is sad…" she wrote, "that the condition of women and children in our factories is getting to be as wretched as Europe…"

Factory workers were forced to work long hours. Often, children less than ten years of age would work more than sixty hours a week in the hot, dusty mills. The workers developed lung problems and other illnesses because they breathed the lint-filled air.

Sarah supported new laws that would limit the number of hours children could work and guaranteed that they would receive at least three months of schooling a year. She knew that such laws would be difficult to enforce, but felt that their passage afforded yet another opportunity for women. Rhode Island, for example, had established a commission, made up of women, to visit the factories and see that its labor laws were being obeyed. Every town that had a mill could do the same, Sarah suggested.

To My Countrywomen

Surprisingly, Sarah still believed that women should not vote. For several years, women called "suffragettes" had worked to convince the government that all adults, men *and* women, should be allowed to vote.

Sarah argued that women would not gain very much even if they voted. Voting, she wrote, would not get a woman a better paying job if she was only suited for a low-paying one. It would not help her deal with family problems. Whether or not she could vote, a woman could accomplish anything she set her mind to. Women didn't need to get involved with politics in order to lead a useful life. Women could influence laws and elections simply by discussing their opinions.

Sarah believed politics often did more to ruin things than help. She pointed to the way politics had destroyed the lives of Native American people. Even while the Civil War was being fought, settlers continued to head west to claim land, farm, and begin new lives. Hundreds of thousands of Native Americans already had been pushed away from their ancestral homes. Sarah looked upon these changes with mixed feelings. She was thrilled when the last rail was set for the Transcontinental Railroad in May of 1869. In Sarah's eyes, this event truly united the whole country. But her heart ached for the displaced Native American women and children.

Later that same year, she published a booklet containing a narrative poem called *Love, or a Woman's Destiny*. The poem expressed many of Sarah's beliefs concerning a woman's place in society. Sarah also used the poem as a way to express some of her political opinions. For example, she did not feel that relations with the Native Americans had been handled fairly. Native American families should be as free and protected as anyone else in the United States:

> "...While the Indian names we cherish
> On the warship, on the state,
> Shall we let their women perish
> Leave the children to their fate?

> Our land opens to all people,
> Flag protects from sea to sky;
> Faith is free by cross and steeple
> Shall we see the red race die?

Sarah believed that a woman influenced others through her love and goodness. She didn't need to, as Sarah wrote, "build the city" or "rule the state." She had spent her life using her pen to influence people's attitudes. She had worked hard to show that women would make good teachers, missionaries, and doctors. But these were all jobs that Sarah felt went along with a woman's caring nature.

Sarah, however, did not approve of women doing just any type of work. She "wouldn't recommend" for example, that women become lawyers. Today we might find such attitudes strange but in Sarah's opinion certain jobs did not go well with feminine nature.

> "Looking back over the past twenty years, we see such rapid strides made in…ideas we…advanced concerning women's needs of better education…there seems now some fear lest she should in eagerness show the world what she can do, aim at doing men's work…This would be a serious mistake."

During this period Sarah also studied the problems of prisoners who returned to crime after their jail sentences were completed. Jails, Sarah felt, should be places where prisoners could learn skills in order to lead useful lives after they were freed. She pointed to a firm in Bridgeport, Connecticut which taught "the

convicts while in prison some mechanical business…
And if faithfully served continue to employ them after
their discharge." She urged companies in other states
to follow their example.

In the summer of 1870 Emma Willard died.
Sarah reminded readers of all that Mrs. Willard had
accomplished in the field of women's education. She
suggested that the school Mrs. Willard had founded,
the Troy Female Seminary be given a new name:
The Emma H. Willard Seminary. Today, the Emma
Willard School continues to be a well-respected college
preparatory school for young women.

In spite of her sadness over Emma's death, Sarah
had many reasons to be content. *Godey's Lady's Book*
was in its fortieth year of publication. The magazine
had survived when may others had not. In the fall,
President Ulysses S. Grant renewed the annual
Thanksgiving proclamation "to a united people…a
nation at peace within itself…" But the holiday was still
not celebrated by law. "Look onward another eighty
years to November, 1950," Sarah wrote, "what will
be the record of our National Thanksgiving Day?" She
could not know, of course, that it would take nearly
that long for her dream to become reality.

Sarah was eighty-four years old in 1871. When asked about retirement she wrote:

> "When I see others look forward to giving up their occupations and spending an old age of idleness, I always think how much happier they would be to work, according to their strength, until the end of their days. For my own part, I hope to spend the remnant of my long life in doing all I can with my pen, in work which I hope will benefit my countrywomen..."

By 1873, the United States was already planning to celebrate its 100th anniversary. An International Exhibition of Arts would be held in Philadelphia. Sarah and Louis Godey were proud of their host city and devoted many pages of the *Lady's Book* to this event. Sarah was especially pleased to note that one entire building would contain arts and crafts created by American women.

The United States was only twelve years old when Sarah was born. In a sense, the lady editor and her country had grown up together. Sarah had seen so many changes, especially in her favorite cause, the

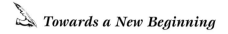

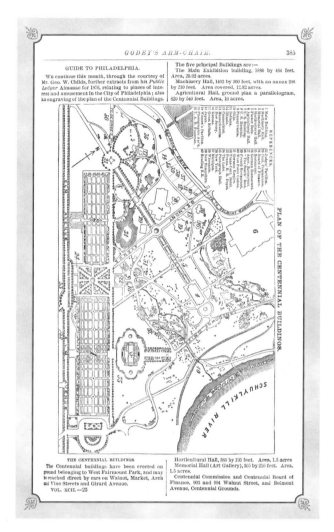

Godey's Lady's Book devoted many pages to preparations for America's centennial celebration.

education of women: "…every state…" she wrote, "has its common school system [and] public and private [schools for women] are numbered by the hundreds."

She had seen new states join the union. The country was now connected from Atlantic to Pacific. Transportation had greatly improved. Sarah was so proud of the United States, she urged women from foreign countries to come to America for the Centennial celebration. She practically guaranteed that they would have a wonderful time. "There is now," she wrote, "no country in which traveling is made for ladies more agreeable than in the United States. Luxuriously furnished steamships…river boats…and sleeping cars and still more palatial hotels receive them on all leading routes."

Louis Godey suffered his own loss the year before the great centennial. In January, 1875, his wife died suddenly. She was well-loved in the Philadelphia community and had been very involved in many works of charity. Following his wife's death, Godey's own health began to fail. He considered retiring as publisher of the *Lady's Book*. Sarah would have to make a decision, too. Perhaps it finally was time for her to leave her editorial duties behind.

Chapter Thirteen

The Last Editorial
1877 – 1879

So many changes occur in society in one hundred years. Sarah had not only seen the United States evolve, she had been instrumental in making many changes happen in her beloved country.

The lady editor was still, at her advanced age, an attractive woman. She followed her own advice about exercising, eating well, and wearing comfortable clothing in styles that suited her personality and figure. She had outlived two of her children but her grandchildren gave her great joy.

Sarah understood Louis Godey's loss following the death of his wife. It was tiring to try to continue one's way of life when death changed so much. She decided that perhaps, she was getting a little tired, too.

Sarah was nearly ninety years old when Louis Godey chose to give up publishing "the Book." The ten years that Sarah had imagined she would spend as a "lady editor" had stretched quietly and forcefully to fifty. She had been associated with Louis Godey for nearly forty of those years. Since the death of her daughter, Josepha, Sarah had done most of her editorial work at home from her large sunny bedroom. Here, she was surrounded by things she loved. Her grandchildren came and went as they pleased, careful not to interrupt Sarah as she worked, but content to sit curled up with good books on the large chintz sofa near her desk.

It was here that Sarah took stock of all the things she had done in her life. She had written about her home and family in Newport, New Hampshire. She had explained that her education came first from her mother, then in the town school, and later with her brother, Horatio. She had described how her husband, David, had encouraged her writing and given her confidence in her talent. How different her life might have been had he lived! Yet, how different many other lives might have been, too. Now it was time to write the last "Editor's Table."

Sarah decided to write about the accomplishments that had given her the most satisfaction. First and foremost was the education of women:

> "My first object in assuming my new position, was to promote the education of my own sex. I believed that the immense importance of this education had never yet been insisted upon; and I believed, moreover, that women were the appointed teachers of the

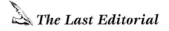

An engraving of the Bunker Hill Monument as it appeared when it was completed in 1843. Sarah was proud of the role women had played in the project.

young…[from] the first number of …
Ladies Magazine…until [it] was merged
with a larger publication, there was not
a volume of it which did not abound in
appeals, in arguments, stories, songs, and
criticisms bearing upon this subject of
feminine education."

She continued this quest when she became editor
of *Godey's Lady's Book.* Her writings had an impact:

"How complete that change has been
all can appreciate. The public schools of
the country, both for boys and girls, are
mainly taught by women; private schools
for girls are almost completely under the
care of ladies…public opinion is that our
children are better taught than in former
times, and that woman, as an instructress
is, at last, in her rightful place…"

Sarah wrote about her pride in the completion of
the Bunker Hill Monument and the part "the ladies"
had played in raising money for its completion. She
reminded readers that it was in the *Lady's Book* that she
had first lobbied for a national day of thanksgiving.

"These efforts have not been fruitless;
and for fourteen years the President has
regularly issued his proclamation fixing a
day for a National Thanksgiving. It needs
now only the sanction of Congress to
make it permanent."

Nearly thirty years had passed since Sarah and
a group of women had formed the Ladies Medical
Missionary Society. Their group had raised funds in
order to educate women doctors who would go to India
and other countries to help less fortunate people. It
had taken years to convince the public that unmarried
women doctors should be allowed to help in foreign
missions.

There was more, much more. Sarah had encouraged
new writers; families had learned from her books;
Mount Vernon now belonged to America's citizens;
the sad years of the great Civil War were over and the
country was truly able to celebrate its Centennial. But
there was only so much space even for this last "Editor's
Table." It was time for Sarah to finish her work.

"...And now, having reached my
ninetieth year, I must bid farewell to my

*Sarah Hale was 91 years old when she died
in Philadelphia in 1879.*

countrywomen…New avenues for higher culture and for good works are opening before them, which fifty years ago were unknown. That they may improve these opportunities, and be faithful to their high vocation, is my heartfelt prayer…

"…Trusting that all our friends who read these lines may share in the fruition of these hopes, and wishing to each and all every blessing that our Heavenly Father can bestow, we bid them an affectionate farewell."

Sarah Josepha Hale
Philadelphia
December 31st, 1877

Sarah spent the remaining year and a half of her life quietly. She died on April 30, 1879. Newspapers all over the country reported on the exceptional life of the country's first woman editor. But while Sarah was pleased with the changes she had helped bring about, she always maintained that she used her pen for her countrywomen.

Chapter Fourteen

Sarah's Work Continues

Sarah Hale's influence is still being felt today, more than one hundred years after her death. She would be pleased to see that cities and towns continue to set aside public play areas for children and that today's children still sing "Mary's Lamb." In the early 1900s, other writers claimed authorship of the poem or said that the events described in the poem had happened to them. Sarah's family did not allow the claims to go unchallenged. Richard Walden Hale, Sarah's grandnephew wrote a rebuttal article in 1904 and reprinted his copy of *Poems for Our Children* in 1916. In 1917, Sarah's granddaughter, Mary Hunter, wrote to a journalist who was investigating the facts:

> "...My Uncle, Horatio Hale, says distinctly that the incident happened to his mother. That settles it, to my mind, for being a lawyer he was exact and careful in his statements."

Sarah herself left proof that she had written the poem. In her book, *Dictionary of Poetical Quotations,* which was published in 1849, she included part of the poem under the theme "Animals" and listed herself as author:

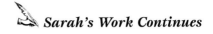

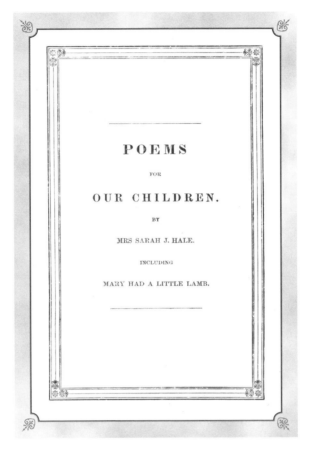

Sarah's grandnephew, Richard Hunter, owned one of three original copies of Poems for Our Children. *He had it reprinted as proof that Sarah had written the poem.*

"And you each gentle animal
In confidence may bind,
And make them follow at your call,
If you are always kind.

Mrs. Hale

Today, women have thousands of choices if they decide to further their education. Sarah might be shocked to learn that women have become everything from prize-winning jockeys to scientists, and yes, even lawyers.

We still read books by authors recommended in Sarah Hale's Literary Notices. Writers such as Charles Dickens, Louisa May Alcott, and Edgar Allan Poe remain popular today. In 1871, Sarah recommended a new book: *The English Governess at the Siamese Court, being Recollections of Six Years in the Royal Palace at Bangkok by Mrs. Leonowans.* Today, many people are more familiar with the award winning musical play that was created from that story: *The King and I.*

Mariner's House continues to welcome visiting seamen to Boston. Sailors still can find food and shelter there. Counseling and educational services are provided. Sarah, a modern thinker during her lifetime, would probably appreciate the fitness center and

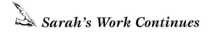

internet connections that the inn now offers.

In 1956 poet Robert Frost received the first Sarah Josepha Hale Award. The award is given annually by the trustees of the Richards Free Library in Sarah's hometown of Newport, New Hampshire. The award is presented to a writer who, like Sarah, is associated with New England. It honors the author's body of work.

Perhaps the thing that would have surprised Sarah most is that it took over one hundred years before her dream of a national day of Thanksgiving became a reality. It would take another great war to make it happen. Not until the middle of World War II did Congress finally pass a law making the fourth Thursday in November a national holiday.

Each year, as we join with our families and friends to celebrate this holiday, we might think of Sarah Hale. She gave our country many reasons to be thankful.

A fashion plate published in
Godey's Lady's Book., *January, 1842.*

A Time Line of
Sarah Josepha Hale's Life

1776— The United States declare their independence from Great Britain.

1783— The Treaty of Paris signed; the American Revolution Ends.

1788— October 24: Sarah Josepha born to Martha and Gordon Buell of Newport, NH.

1789— George Washington becomes the first President of the United States.

1805— Sarah's brother, Horatio Buell, leaves Newport for Dartmouth College.

1810— Sarah's family sells their farm and opens the Rising Sun Tavern in Newport.

1811— David Hale moves to Newport.
Sarah's mother and younger sister die.

1813— October 23: Sarah marries David Hale.

1815— The Hales' first son, David, is born.

1817— The Hales' second son, Horatio, is born.

(Note: dates in **bold** print show some events in United States History)

1818— Sarah becomes seriously ill.

1819— Sarah's third child, Frances Ann, is born.

1820— The Hales' fourth child, Josepha, is born.
**The American colony, Liberia, is
started in Africa.**

1822— September 25: Sarah's husband, David
Hale dies of pneumonia.
The Hales' fifth child, William, is born.
**Henry Dearborn proposes plans
for The Bunker Hill Monument.**

1823— Sarah publishes *The Genius of Oblivion and
Other Original Poems.*

**1825— The cornerstone for the Bunker Hill
Monument is laid.**

1827— Sarah's first novel, *Northwood, or, Life
North and South* is published.
John Blake asks Sarah to edit his *Ladies
Magazine.*

1828— The first issue of *Ladies Magazine* is
launched.

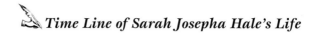

1829— Sarah Hale moves to Boston.

1830— The first fashion plates are published
in *Ladies Magazine*.
"Mary's Lamb" appears in *Poems for Our Children*.
Godey's Lady's Book is published in
Philadelphia.

1831— Lowell Mason publishes *Juvenile Lyre*…
and puts Mary's Lamb to music.

1832— The Seamen's Aid Society is founded.

1833— Sarah's son David graduates from
West Point.
Horatio Hale enters Harvard.

1834— The *Ladies Magazine* changes its name
to *American Ladies Magazine*.
Sarah becomes part-owner of *American Ladies Magazine*.

1836— The Seamen's Aid Society opens its
first store.
John Blake agrees to sell *American Ladies Magazine* to Louis Godey.

1837— Sarah begins editing the combined *American Ladies* and *Godey's Lady's Book*.

1838— Horatio Hale joins the United States Exploring Expedition.

1839— Emma Willard marries, then leaves, Dr. Christopher Yates.

Sarah's son, David Hale dies while stationed at the Canadian border.

1840— The "Women's Fair" at Fanueil Hall raises over $30,000 for the Bunker Hill Monument.

1841— Sarah Hale moves to Philadelphia.

January: *Godey's Lady's Book* becomes the first magazine to publish an issue written entirely by women.

Edgar Allan Poe becomes editor of *Graham's Lady's and Gentleman's Magazine*.

1842— Sarah writes a column suggesting a national day of Thanksgiving.

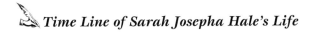

Emma Willard publishes *History of the United States.*

1843— The Bunker Hill Monument is completed.

1844— Frances Ann Hale marries Doctor Lewis Hunter. Sarah moves in with the Hunters on Locust Street in Philadelphia.

1846— *Godey's Lady's Book* supports western migration with a new department: Godey's Model Cottage.

1848— Elizabeth Blackwell becomes the first woman doctor.
Gold is discovered at Sutter's Mill, California. The Gold Rush begins.
Elizabeth Cady Stanton and others hold a convention to discuss women's voting rights in Seneca Falls, New York.

1849— The Ladies Education Society sends 100 teachers to start schools in California.

1850— Godey's Lady's Book is twenty years old.
**Congress develops the Compromise
of 1850 to try to keep peace
between slave owners
and abolitionists.**

1852— **Harriet Beecher Stowe publishes**
Uncle Tom's Cabin.
**All United States Territories and
all but two states share a national
Thanksgiving.**
Sarah reprints *Northwood or, Life North
and South.*

1853— Sarah Hale publishes *Liberia: or,
Mr. Peyton's Experiments.*

1855— *Godey's Lady's Book* and the *Southern
Literary Journal* work together to
promote the purchase of Mount
Vernon—the former home of George
Washington.

1860— February: The Mount Vernon Ladies
Society buys Mount Vernon

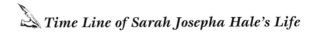

Florence Nightingale publishes a book on practical nursing.

November: Abraham Lincoln elected President of the United States.

December: South Carolina secedes from the Union.

1861— The American Civil War begins.

1863— May: S. Josepha Hale dies at her girls' school.

September: Sarah writes a letter to Abraham Lincoln requesting a national Thanksgiving Day holiday.

November: Lincoln signs the first proclamation naming the fourth Thursday in November a national day of Thanksgiving.

1865— April 9: The Civil War ends. April 15: Abraham Lincoln is assassinated.

1866— Sarah writes editorials about jobs for widowed and single women.

1869— The Transcontinental Railroad is completed

Sarah publishes *Love, or a Woman's Destiny*.

1870— Emma Willard dies.

1875— Louis Godey's wife dies.

1876— Philadelphia hosts a Centennial celebration.

1877— Louis Godey retires.
Sarah writes her last editorial.

1879— April 30: Sarah Hale dies.

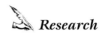 *Research*

Research Conducted At

The Richards Library
58 North Main Street
Newport, New Hampshire

The Boston Public Library
Rare Book Division
700 Boylston Street
Boston, MA 02116

The Library of Congress
101 Independence Ave. SE
Washington, D. C. 20540

The Historical Society of Pennsylvania
1300 Locust Street
Philadelphia, PA 19107-5699

Special thanks to:
Nancy Iannucci, The Emma Willard School
Eric Frazier, Patricia Feeley, Boston Public Library
Andrea Thorpe, Richards Free Library, Newport, NH

Selected Bibliography

Finley, Ruth E. *The Lady of Godey's.* Philadelphia: J.B. Lippencott & Company, 1931.

Fryatt, Norma R. *Sarah Josepha Hale: The Life and Times of a Nineteenth-Century Career Woman.* New York: Hawthorne Books, Inc. 1975.

Hale, Richard Walden. " 'Mary Had a Little Lamb' and Its Author." *Century Magazine.* March 1904: 738 – 742.

Hale, Sarah J. *The Genius of Oblivion and Other Original Poems.* Concord, NH: Jacob B. Moore, 1823.

Hale, Sarah J. *Northwood; or, Life North and South Showing the True Character of Both.* (Reprint Edition) New York: H. Long & Brother: 1852.

Hale, Sarah J. *Liberia; or, Mr. Peyton's Experiment.* New York: Harper & Brothers, Publishers: 1853.

Hale, Sarah J. *Flora's Interpreter and Fortuna Flora.* Boston: Chase, Nichols, and Hill, 1860.

Hale, Sarah J. editor. *A Complete Dictionary of Poetical Quotations.* Philadelphia: J. B. Lippincott, 1861.

Hale, Sarah J. *Woman's Record; or, Sketches of all Distinguished Women* (Third Revised Edition) New York: Harper & Brothers, 1870.

Hale, Sarah J. *The Good Housekeeper.* (Reprint of 1841 edition) Mineoloa, New York: Dover Publications, 1996.

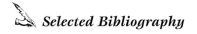

Selected Bibliography

History of Newport, New Hampshire from 1766-1878 (with a genealogical register by Edmund Wheeler) Concord, NH: The Republican Press Association, 1879.

Lossing, Benson J. *George Washington's Mount Vernon, or, Mount Vernon and its Associations, Historical Biographical, and Pictorial.* (Reprint of 1870 edition) New York: The Fairfax Press, 1983.

Mason, Lowell. *Juvenile Lyre: or, Hymns and Songs, Religious, Moral, and Cheerful, Set to Appropriate Music, for the Use of Primary and Common Schools.* Boston: Richardson, Lord & Holbrook, 1831.

Osgood, Charles and Samuel, editors. *The New Hampshire Book, Being Specimens of the Literature of the Granite State.* Nashville, NH: Charles T. Gill, 1844.

Page, Thomas Nelson. *History and Preservation of Mount Vernon.* (revised edition) New York: The Knickerbocker Press, 1932.

Radcliffe, Ann. *The Mysteries of Udolpho, a Romance; Interspersed with some Pieces of Poetry.* (Contemporary reprint of original 1794 edition) New York: Oxford University Press, 1980.

Index

[ ] = illustrations

Index

[ ] = illustrations

[ ] = illustrations

[ ] = illustrations

About the Author

Muriel L. Dubois a native of New Hampshire,
is the award-winning author of *Abenaki Captive*
a novel based on an incident in the life of
Revolutionary war General John Stark.
In addition, she has written over
30 non-fiction books for children.
Visit her site at www.murieldubois.com